CAREER
by Design

A Career Guide to Help Students, Veterans, &
Career Changers Find Their Dream Job and
Succeed Once They Find It

CAREER

by Design

A Career Guide to Help Students, Veterans, &
Career Changers Find Their Dream Job and
Succeed Once They Find It

An easy to follow career planner with actionable steps how to
choose a career you'll love, land the job you want, and make the
kind of money to live the kind of life most only dream about!

Ron Willbanks

https://www.facebook.com/CareerByDesign2019

https://www.linkedin.com/in/ronwillbanks/

Ordering Information: Special discounts are available on quantity purchases by schools, colleges, governmental institutions, and private associations.

Printed in the United States of America

First Printing, 2019

Jacket design by Eric Bookout

ISBN 978-1-7337748-0-2 (paperback)
ISBN 978-1-7337748-1-9 (ebook)

DEDICATION

This book is dedicated to young people—high school, trade school, or college students—seeking advice on how to figure out what type of job will make them happy. It is also for not-so-young people who may have stumbled out of the gate on their first attempt and need a second (or third) chance at finding a fulfilling their dream.

As a veteran, I also wanted to provide a career guide for returning soldiers, sailors, airmen, marines, and coasties who want to find out what their options are as they plan for their new, second life as a civilian.

I'm hoping this book will help you plan your career so you can be successful sooner rather than later. Regardless of whether you are doing things the easy way or the harder way, this book can help you plan for a career that can create a better life for you and your family.

TABLE OF CONTENTS

Foreword   ii
Introduction   iv

FIGURING OUT YOUR DREAM CAREER

1 – Getting More Out of Life   1
2 – Employee vs. Entrepreneur   9
   Being an Employee   10
   Becoming an Entrepreneur   13
3 – Creating Your Plan   18
4 – Career Options   26
   Trade Schools   29
   Art and Design   37
   Business   39
   STEM (Science, Technology, Engineering, & Mathematics)   45
   Information Technology (IT)   50
   Project Management   56
   Military Service   57

FINDING A JOB

5 – Targeting Your Desired Job   64
   Creating Your Resume   68
6 – Interviewing Skills   76
   Interview Questions   82
7 – Communication Skills   94

SUCCEEDING IN YOUR JOB

8 – Traits of Successful People   102
   Behaviors of Successful People   102
   Behaviors that Impede Success   112
9 – Master Your Profession   121
10 – Making Your Boss Successful   132
   Types of Bosses   137
   Managing Up   141

STAYING SUCCESSFUL

11 – Pay Yourself First   148
12 – Continual Self-Improvement   154
Reading List   160
Works Cited   161

FOREWORD

I took the liberty of having two forewords. The first one is written by someone who changed careers at thirty-eight years old. The second is written by someone who has been in the same career field for his whole career. I hope you find their perspectives interesting.

You picked up this book because you are already a little excited, a little curious as to the possibilities for your future. Can I do it? Am I too young? Is it too late for me? Where do I start? Read this book. It's well researched and thoughtfully written by someone who faced these same questions himself, and helped others answer these questions during his tenure as a recruiter.

You may be thinking of just making a change in your life or pursuing a truly transformational dream unrealized. Maybe you are fresh out of school and wondering what you will do with your life, or maybe you are at a crossroads in your career, looking to better your lot in life for the benefit of you and your family. This book will help you take stock of your current situation, develop a strategy and execute a plan to shape your future.

Ron Willbanks and I have been friends for 25 years. His heart and soul are woven into the following chapters, reflected in the encouraging tone and helpful strategies. An honest book written by an honest man is at your fingertips right now to help you take that next step. The rest is up to you.

— Michael Gibbs, Esq.

Over the course of my sales career, I have had the opportunity to interact with thousands of accomplished professionals from all over the world. When I first meet someone, I tend to ask a few questions to break the ice, such as "Do you love what you do?" or "Do you do what you love?" Interestingly, I could probably count the number of times I heard "I do what I love" on one hand. I think that's unfortunate.

Imagine for a moment how happy you could be if you took the time to evaluate what you love to do and decided to actually pursue your dream job. In my own career, nobody took the time to help me understand what I needed to do today to achieve my future goals tomorrow. Even though I've been very successful in my career, I wonder how things might've been different if I'd created a game plan to develop my skills, broaden my network, and plot a deliberate course towards what I wanted to achieve.

In the more than 25 years I have known Ron Willbanks, he has been more than a friend. He has been a colleague, confidant, and has counseled me on a number of my personal career decisions. He holds himself to a high standard and, like many of us who want to achieve, he wants more. The difference is he takes the time to develop his plan and is courageous enough to pursue his dreams.

In the following pages, he covers the often-overlooked aspects of career choice and progression. The lesson is simple: take the time to create a career plan so you can do what you love to do and enjoy a fulfilling career. That way, it'll never feel like work. Once pointed in the right direction, continue to invest in yourself. If you know where you want to go and make the plan to get there, your chances for living the kind of life you want to live are much better.

Do you want to do what you love? If your answer is yes, then take the first step and read on.

— Sean Harris

INTRODUCTION

Human nature compels us to improve ourselves. When you are young, you want to make your mark on the world, to distinguish yourself, and make a difference. Everyone is unique and has their own personal source of motivation. Some of you possess a natural, inner drive to excel, a competitive spirit to win, or hunger to reach your full potential. Others are motivated by a desire to make someone they love proud or need to get out of an unhappy situation.

Most high-school students don't know what they want to do when they graduate. Are you going to attend college? Do you plan on enrolling in a vocational or trade school? Will you join the military? If you are a college freshman or sophomore, you are probably wrestling with the decision on what you should major in . . . and *career* is something you'll worry about at graduation. What's more, you haven't even thought about putting together a *career* plan . . . much less a *life* plan. You may be feeling the pressure about all the unknowns and don't know where to start.

If the questions above are similar to the ones you are struggling with, this book will help you. I will guide you through the steps on how to design your dream career path—one that can make you happy *and* earn enough money so you can live the kind of lifestyle you want.

My goal in writing this book is to offer you a useful guide that is easy to read and provides an easy-to-follow roadmap to help you design your career path. In each chapter, I provide tools and tips you can incorporate into your tool belt. I also wrote this guide to be something you could read in a day or so . . . and yet still provide enough information on the vast array of career choices available and the range of specialties within each field.

I explain ways to help you unearth your individual strengths and how to fit them into your career plan—whether it's working for someone else or working for yourself. Regardless of which path you take, you need a plan because *"hope"* is not a good strategy. You can't *wish* your way to success. You need to know how to figure things out—to methodically think things through so you can increase your chances of achieving success.

While this guide is flexible enough to help young people entering the workforce for the first time, it can also assist veterans returning from military service or those who are a little older (and wiser) in making a career change. Who wouldn't like a do-over, right?

Likewise, this book is not just for those who plan to attend college because *college is not for everybody*. You can find your way to success by attending a vocational or trade school, working as an apprentice to become a trade journeyman, and more.

This book is organized to help career-seekers and career-changers work through the process to determine how to make a good choice to earn a living, create a resume that pops, and prepare for a job interview. It also provides advice on how to be successful once you get a job. You'll benefit from my experience as a recruiter early in my career and my thirty-five years of management experience as I share essential tips on how to distinguish yourself from your peers, get the promotion, and earn the biggest raises. I provide examples to illustrate how to avoid preventable mistakes that could hinder your career advancement. It is my intent to have a copy of this book available for every high-school student, college student, or returning veteran who needs help with deciding on a career choice.

Not everyone is lucky enough to have a trusted mentor help them figure things out. It is my sincere hope this book can help you avoid losing valuable time using the trial-and-error method to decide on your career path. *Time* is something you can never get back. This guide can jump start your planning process and help you make better decisions and put you in charge of designing your future. Start the journey today toward maximizing your potential . . . Good luck!

Figuring Out Your Dream Career

1 – GETTING MORE OUT OF LIFE

*"All our dreams can come true if
we have the courage to pursue them."
– Walt Disney*

If you want more out of life, you will have to make up your mind to go for it. If you want something badly enough, don't let anyone or anything stop you from achieving your goals. For those who are brave enough to pursue their dreams, you will be rewarded. As you read this, however, be forewarned that nothing in life is guaranteed.

I wish we all had a crystal ball so we could look ahead to see how everything turns out. But there's no such thing. In reality, you can't possibly predict how everything will turn out five or ten years from now. This is especially true if you don't plan for it. On the other hand, if you decide to take control of your destiny, you will need to create a plan for how you want to live your life. If you do this, your odds of achieving success increase exponentially.

Perhaps you've heard the saying "nothing in life worth having is easy." While that's mostly true, take heart, because once your mind is made up, you'll find there is nothing that can stop you. Even if you fail at some task along your chosen journey, you'll consider it a temporary setback and compartmentalize it as a *life lesson*. You'll learn from it and push on.

For those seeking guidance from this book, understand this is not the complete, unabridged secret to life. I wrote this book to supplement—not replace—advice your parents, family, guidance counselor, or other trusted people in your life can provide. Ultimately, however, YOU are responsible for your life and must make the final decision of how you want your story to go.

So I highly recommend you DREAM BIG. You *do* want to have a *great* life, right? Once you are out there in the world living on your own, I assume you want to have at least enough income to live comfortably. If you're reading this book, I also can imagine you want to enjoy some of the good things in life—whether that's a reliable car, nice home, fashionable clothes, beach vacation, or all of the above. Envision yourself doing something you can be passionate about. Create a picture in your mind, and imagine where you want to be one day.

Perhaps you are motivated by the need to take care of loved ones in your family or want a family of your own. If you want a family someday, you'll probably want them to live in a safe neighborhood with good schools where your children can blossom. It's only natural you'd want to provide the best of everything for your loved ones . . . to have a happy life filled with adventure. You want your children to have all the advantages you wish you had growing up. Then the daydream fades and the question pops up in your head, "How the heck am I going to pull this off?" Is there a system or repeatable roadmap I can follow to achieve success?

If you don't have all the answers yet you can take solace in the fact that you're not alone. The vast majority of us didn't have everything going for us while growing up either. I assume you weren't born with a silver spoon in your mouth and didn't have the perfect mentor guiding you as you grew up. As for me, I didn't graduate at the top of my class and was far from having everything figured out at eighteen years old—much less at twenty-one. If you feel a little lost and could use some advice on how to build a successful career and a happy life, then I am here to help.

As a more seasoned citizen, I have seen a lot of what works and what does not. I've made some mistakes early in life that set me back. If you are young and haven't made any serious mistakes yet, please read on. If you're a little older, that's the bad news . . . The good news is you are a little wiser too. Now is a good day to take charge and design the kind of life you want. Besides, it's not how you start; it's how you finish, right?

"So many of our dreams at first seem impossible,
then they seem improbable, and then, when we summon
the will, they soon become inevitable."
– Christopher Reeve

DREAMS ARE A WONDERFUL THING

Dreams can be a great motivator. I believe most people dream about having the life they want and the things they believe will bring them happiness. Dreams bring you joy and cause you to fantasize about how you will achieve your goals. In fact, this is how most successful people start out. They have *dreams* that lead to developing *ambition* . . . that leads to awakening *desire*, which become *actions*, and ultimately, becomes your way of life.

Many young people growing up in America fantasize about being a movie star, famous musician, or professional athlete. When I was young, I wanted to be a lead singer / guitar player in a rock band. I would dream of playing songs that rose to Number One on the music charts. My problem: I never did anything about it. After graduating high school, I played a little guitar with my cousin (who was more gifted than I was) but did not pursue it. We even had a couple guys who were part owners of a local bar that heard us play and offered to help us cut a demo, but we didn't follow up. We were too lazy and afraid of failure. Yet, for a long time afterward, whenever a great rock song would play on the radio, I would sink back and daydream about what might have been.

For several years, I thought about taking music lessons . . . but between work, night school, and whatever other excuses I could muster, I never followed through. Many years later, I realized I had done nothing to pursue that dream and finally understood why. I didn't want it badly enough to do something about it. Oh sure, I would have loved to have been a famous rock star jet-setting around the world living the good life, but I did nothing about it. I didn't even try hard enough to fail. Learn from my mistake. Find your passion . . . your purpose . . . your *desire* . . . and *do something* about it.

"If you wait, all that happens is you get older."
– Larry McMurtry

Okay, your response may initially be "I don't know how" or "I'm afraid" or "It's too hard." Fear not. You can learn how to overcome your fears so you can figure it out. When you were a baby and tried to learn to walk, did you quit after you fell the first time? No. You tried and tried again until you could stand. You probably fell at least a hundred times before successfully taking your first step. Despite all your prior failures, you persevered and, eventually, taught yourself to walk.

Things are not so different as an adult—except now, you have a fear of failure that paralyzes you. Before you create your plan, you have to be honest with yourself. *How badly do you want to change your life?* Then comes an even tougher question: "What are you willing to *sacrifice* to get what you want?" Do you have a fire in your belly? How intense is your desire? Is it more powerful than doing nothing? Better than watching TV? Better than playing video games? Better than spending countless hours on social media or texting your friends? Are you willing to give up sitting around watching TV, sleeping in, or partying all the time?

To achieve anything in life, you will have to muster enough passion and desire to overcome the laws of physics—i.e., a couch potato will remain at rest unless induced to change its state by an opposing force. The opposing force is ambition. This may sound funny to you, but it's true. Are you willing to do what it takes to defeat apathy, laziness, and a propensity to procrastinate?

To help you wrestle with this life-changing question, I provide a simple decision-making tool to help you decide if it's worth it to you. It's a proven method that I believe Benjamin Franklin created to help him with the decision-making process. It is known as a *Pros and Cons* list. I took the liberty of adding columns labeled "Impact" next to the Pros and Cons so you can think about the impact of choosing one path over the other.

PRO	IMPACT	CON	IMPACT
What benefits will I enjoy if I act on my DESIRE to live my life the way I want to?	Write down the consequences of taking control of my destiny.	What will happen if I take the EASY path and do not give it my all to succeed?	Write down the consequences if I allow others to shape my future.

Figure 1: Pros & Cons Tool – What is Your Purpose?

The question you need to answer is: "What will happen if I decide to take control of my life to achieve my dreams?" Be honest with yourself and take some time to think about the kind of life you want to live. Fill in the advantages and disadvantages for each Pro and Con, then fill out the Impact columns. If you need more space for your answers, re-create the tool on a bigger piece of paper. I believe you'll find this will help you define what your _purpose_ is with a bit more clarity.

After you complete the table, read it to yourself aloud. What are you telling yourself? If you are thinking along the lines, "Of course it is better to take control of my life . . ." that's precisely the point. You need to realize this, understand it completely, and live it.

It will require a good measure of personal discipline. However, once you have made up your mind, it actually becomes easier over time. Once you possess the resolve to defeat the law of inertia, you will be able to overcome any obstacles that come your way. More importantly, you will feel proud of yourself because you know you're doing the things you're supposed to be doing to improve your life.

> *"The starting point of*
> *all achievement is desire."*
> *– Napoleon Hill*

MISERY LOVES COMPANY

You may find there are people you know who do not have aspirations like you do. Even if some do, most are still not willing to put in the work and make the sacrifices it takes to achieve their dreams. Sadly, the vast majority of people don't have much drive to better their lives. If you share your dreams with them, you may even hear some of your friends or family respond by describing all the reasons why you will not succeed. Doubters are quick to rain on your parade and all too enthusiastically point out why your idea is a bad idea. It's amazing how creative these naysayers can be when coming up with ways why your dream just isn't practical.

You may also find close friends and family trying to hold you back for other reasons. Perhaps they don't want you to outgrow them and leave them behind. On the other hand, there are times your skeptics are well-meaning loved ones who genuinely believe you're making a big mistake to take such a risk. To protect you, they try to talk you out of pursuing your dream because they don't want to see you fail. Despite their good intentions, they can't make such an important decision for you.

Some years ago, a good friend of mine quit a decent paying job as an operations manager of a biotech company. For years, he secretly pined away at the thought of becoming a lawyer. At that time, he was thirty-eight years old. When he finally made up his mind to go for it, he told some of his closest friends he was quitting his job to go to law school. They laughed. Even some of his family members told him it was not a good decision. His brother told him there were too many lawyers in the world already. None of this talk deterred him. His wife believed in him and—more importantly—he believed in himself. She encouraged him to pursue his dream and assured him she would support them both while he attended law school full time.

It's a good thing he didn't listen to his skeptics and instead listened to his own counsel (pun intended). In his final year, he worked himself into a clerkship at a prestigious law firm and later landed a job with that firm upon graduation. He worked long hours, but within five years after graduating, he was offered a position with one of their clients as the general counsel of a national restaurant chain. Not bad, eh?

The lesson to learn here is—when making a life-changing decision—nobody knows all the specifics that factor into your decision as well as you do. No one else knows how much importance you place on certain considerations—including your spouse or best friends. In the end, YOU have to make the decision that is right for you, and then commit to your decision. Life will throw plenty of challenges your way to test your mettle. However, once your mind is made up and you have committed yourself down the right path, you may be surprised at how much your resolve strengthens the closer you get to achieving your goals.

RAMIFICATIONS OF DOING NOTHING

Trying to get ahead in life is tough. It's like swimming to shore against a rip current. What options do you have? Consider the alternative of doing nothing to plan for your future. This can help put your priorities into the proper perspective. If you do nothing to try to get ahead in life, the important question to ask yourself is "Who will I be hurting if I DON'T succeed?"

Let's fast forward ten years into the future and assume whatever path you chose led you to become very successful. Think about what you are able to do because you are prosperous. Since you are successful, you and your family live in a nice, safe neighborhood with good schools, and your children are able to enjoy the benefits those better schools offer. You are able to travel the world to see things most people only dream about. You buy your parents a new home or pay off their mortgage so they can retire with security. In addition, you are able to support the worthy charity or special cause you care about so much.

On the other hand, if you don't strive to reach your potential, none of this will be possible. By exploring the option of doing nothing, you can see the decision of whether to improve your lot in life or not doesn't just affect you. If you don't try to be the best you can be, you won't be just cheating yourself . . . You will be cheating everyone who depends on you. You will be denying your loved ones the great life that could have been theirs. So what do you want to do? Are you going to be a smashing success so you can be happy AND leave a legacy for your family? If so, you'll be glad to know there is more than one right way to do it.

In the next chapter, I'll cover two of the most common ways to be successful. Specifically, I'll describe what it's like to be an employee versus an entrepreneur. While most of us are employees—i.e., we work for an employer—employees can enjoy a rewarding career and be highly compensated. If being an employee is your preferred choice, I'll walk you through how to create a career plan to get a job in the industry of your choice. In comparison, I'll provide a glimpse of what it's like to become a business owner. Rest assured, whatever path you choose, you can achieve success.

2 – EMPLOYEE VS. ENTREPRENEUR

"I am not what happened to me . . .
I am what I choose to become."
– Carl Jung

Do you want to work for someone else or work for yourself? One is not necessarily better than the other. I suppose your answer depends upon your perspective.

The majority of workers are employees, and the top 5 or 10 percent work their way up to executive positions. In general, employees prefer the structure and comradery the corporate world provides. The majority of people want no part of having the responsibility for everything it takes to run their own business. In fact, only about 13 to 16 percent of the labor force owns their own business. The small percentage of business owners typically choose to be entrepreneurs because they want to control their own destiny, don't want to put a limit on how much money they can earn, and/or cannot abide living their life under someone else's rules. Only you can decide what is right for you.

The good news is you can become very successful either way. An important lesson I learned later in life is there is more than one RIGHT way to do things. You cannot discount one approach over another without taking into consideration all the facts associated with a particular situation. For instance, Walmart's founder, Sam Walton, succeeded with a strategy of building stores in rural areas and charging hyper-discounted prices in order to generate high-volume sales with low profit margins. John Nordstrom's strategy was to open a chain of luxury department stores located primarily in urban areas and charge top dollar for exclusive, pricy merchandise. I think we can agree both are very successful.

In this chapter, I show you how you can be successful regardless of what path you design to get there. I present two stories to illustrate how your journey might unfold if you decide to work for someone else or become your own boss. The protagonists are Barrett, the employee, and Camryn, the entrepreneur. In both accounts, I uncover some of the likely challenges and obstacles they, like you, would inevitably face.

Being an Employee

Working as a W-2 employee is what we normally think of as a typical wage earner. As an employee, you can work for an organization that is for-profit or non-profit as well as a private company or a public institution. As an employee, you are typically paid salary or hourly wages, provided benefits such as health insurance and paid time off, and work hours that are determined by your employer.

The majority of people prefer the "security" they believe comes with working for someone else—whether that is a small, local business or a Fortune 500 company. Perhaps the allure of working with a group of like-minded people is appealing to you. You may also be drawn by the companionship that being part of a team brings. Going to lunch every day with your crew has its appeal. In the long-term, working as a W-2 employee doesn't mean you cannot or will not become successful. Indeed, those with leadership skills can move up to the executive floor, get a corner office, a nice fat salary, plenty of perks, and maybe even a company car.

For this story, our protagonist is Barrett, who is sixteen years old, getting ready to begin his junior year of high school. He dreams of becoming a mechanical engineer and wants to design next-generation engines that are super fuel-efficient and *fast*. As a child, his Uncle Pete gave him a ride in his Porsche 911 through some twisty Hill Country back roads. What a thrill! Since then, Barrett fell in love with the rear-engine 911 and dreams of working for Porsche.

He watches motorsports on TV and fantasizes about being a part of all that someday. He tells his friends at school he is going to work for Porsche someday, and while they are supportive, he feels like they don't really take him seriously. But that doesn't discourage him. In fact, deep inside, he uses it as motivation because one day he WILL achieve his dream.

After dinner one day, he does some research on the Internet to see which colleges have the best engineering schools. If he is going to work for Porsche—whose headquarters is in Stuttgart, Germany—he figures he'll have to learn German. Barrett narrows his search of top engineering schools with ones that have student exchange programs in Germany. He makes a short list of schools and begins researching admission requirements. It looks like he'll have to be in the top 10 to 15 percent academically in his graduating class with a GPA (Grade Point Average) of at least 3.6 or better. His SAT or ACT score will also need to be in the top quartile to meet the minimum admissions requirements for the schools on his list.

Thankfully, his grades are already good; he has a 3.7 GPA so far. Next, Barrett focuses on taking prep courses for the SAT. His dad always says, "Practice makes perfect," and "Preparedness breeds confidence," so he takes practice test after practice test until his practice exam scores consistently result in what could be the top 10 percent. In addition, his physics teacher recommended he take practice exams from different sources because one version of the test may be harder and the other one easier. He thinks this is good advice because he doesn't want to be overconfident and underprepared by taking practice exams that are too easy . . . nor does he want to be disillusioned into quitting if he scores too low on some overly difficult practice exams.

Barrett asks his Uncle Pete for advice too. His uncle confirms he is on the right track and recommends he meet with a guidance counselor at his high school to ask what else he needs to do to be accepted at the school of his choice. He meets with his counselor, who tells him the top schools are looking for well-rounded students with a broad range of interests, which admissions representatives use as predictors of success. Other factors they consider are community service and extracurricular activities. Barrett volunteers at a local middle school as a math tutor, adjusts his schedule to take a German foreign language class, and joins the German Club.

Fast forward to Barrett's second semester of his freshman year in college. He was accepted to the school that was his third choice from his top-ten list and now realizes he was lucky to get into such a great program. He has made some great new friends! He also has taken the initiative to meet with his professors to make sure he is doing the right things to succeed in their classes. In addition, he lets his professors know of his dream to work at Porsche and his willingness to accept any advice they might offer. He takes in all the information he can because he will filter through it to determine what fits best with his personality, goals, and plans.

In his sophomore year, Barrett's networking pays off. One of his college classmates, Yonatan, tells him his brother has a friend who is in the pit crew at an upcoming GT race, and he can get him a pit pass to meet some of the crew. Barrett goes to the race with William and is introduced to some technicians and engineers on the Porsche motorsports teams. He has a million questions and asks for advice on how to become part of Porsche Motorsport. They are gracious and give him some pointers.

Back at school, Barrett continues his studies and keeps in touch with his expanding network of contacts. He arranges to spend his junior year as an exchange student at the University of Stuttgart in Germany. Through the contacts he made at the Le Mans race, he is able to get a warm introduction to the managing director of the Porsche Motorsport Junior Programme. Through the friendships he has made, he even manages to get a little track time at Porsche's test track in Weissach, Germany. When he graduates, he lands a six-month internship as a Praktikant/in Motorkonstruktion (Trainee, Engine Design).

So far, Barrett has done everything he can think of to put himself in a position to succeed. Now it's up to him to impress his superiors with his smarts and work ethic. Will he land a permanent role with Porsche? Time will tell, but I like his chances . . .

Becoming an Entrepreneur

Becoming an entrepreneur takes a lot of gumption. It isn't for everyone. Most people don't know how to open their own business or prefer to be just an employee because it's easier. That said, being an employee at first isn't a bad idea, either. For example, if you want to become an architect and design the tallest skyscrapers in the world, it would be wise to learn your craft with one of the established firms before going out on your own. Likewise, if you want to be an accountant, then working for one of the Big Four accounting firms may be a way to gain some valuable experience early in your career.

But what if you are not one of those people? What if you prefer to march to the beat of your own drum? What if you don't want to have a boss because you want to blaze your own trail? You are creative, full of energy, and a risk-taker. Perhaps the phrase "if you are not living on the edge, you are taking up too much room" has special meaning for you. If you are a great communicator, passionate and possess an ability to connect with people . . . you could have what it takes to be a successful entrepreneur. Besides, half the battle is convincing others to your way of thinking. Does this sound like you? If so, you may very well possess some of the essential qualifications to be an entrepreneur.

Let's look at the story of Camryn, who wants to be an entrepreneur. Her dream is to own her own clothing store. She even knows what she's going to call it—*Chez Camryn!* She daydreams about the beautiful storefront she'll have in the shopping district with her latest fashions displayed in the shop window. In her mind's eye, her store will be chic and edgy, and everyone will want to come to *Chez Camryn!* for the latest fashions.

But where does she start? There is no single, right way to be successful, remember? Let's choose a path that seems to have the least risk. Camryn is realistic enough to comprehend she won't learn it all overnight. She understands it may take years before she gets enough experience to learn the basic aspects on how to run a retail business.

For starters, Camryn decides to look for a job in a clothing store similar to the kind of the store she wants to open. In this way, she can study how to run a retail business from the bottom up. This will enable her to get exposure to details like fashion basics, textiles, proper fit, popular designers, merchandising, store layout, and how to put together outfits that look great and sell. On someone else's dime, she can gain valuable knowledge on how to select and purchase product, manage inventory, run a cash register, and take deposits to the bank. She can also acquire valuable skills like how to upsell, handle returns, deal with theft, and train new employees.

She takes an entry-level sales job with a department store in her hometown. After a few years, Camryn works her way up to store manager. Now, the thought of opening her own business isn't as daunting as before. She never gave up on her dream. Even though she is a little afraid of the unknown, she is courageous and willing to try. She knows she can do this and has a strong, supporting cast of colleagues, friends, and family. She believes in herself. Now that she has experience and some confidence, she also realizes she doesn't have to re-invent the wheel.

Camryn starts talking with other retail store owners who have shops similar in size that appear to be successful and are well established. She assures them she isn't planning to open a boutique next-door to them and finds most proprietors are happy to share their success stories. They tell her some of the smart moves they have made as well as the mistakes they regret and how to avoid them. She also finds she doesn't have to necessarily limit her research to retail clothing store owners. In fact, quite by accident, she has a great conversation with a local carwash owner, Shane. He has three locations and shared some great tips on how to market her store locally if she wants to expand someday.

She takes her father's advice and makes an appointment with a lawyer to discuss what kind of business entity is right for her—i.e., sole proprietorship, partnership, Limited Liability Company (LLC), S-Corp, or C-Corporation. After consulting with the lawyer, he suggests she meet with a CPA (Certified Public Accountant). Even though she has picked up on many of the essentials of bookkeeping through school and work, a CPA is an expert who can help her set up a business entity that fits what she is trying to do and assist her with cash flow management, accounting, and tax planning.

Camryn finds other resources at her disposal such as the Small Business Administration, local colleges and universities, banks, friends, and family. Her aunt tells her their local city hall has an economic development department whose primary purpose is to help new start-ups. She also finds organizations that will help women-owned (as well as minority-owned) businesses with advice, mentoring, and funding support.

She must decide whether to lease or buy a property. She's just starting out and finds even though she has been saving for years, she is cash poor when it comes to capital. Her CPA recommends the best option, for now, is to lease retail space. Her lawyer helps her understand the contract language in a typical retail space lease agreement and suggests she negotiate a non-compete clause so another store can't open next to hers that could cannibalize her sales.

Having talked with other business owners and store managers, she has a reasonable guesstimate of how much her utility bills might be. Her mother recommends she get a real estate inspector to do a walk-through so she won't be unpleasantly surprised to find mold, faulty electrical work, plumbing leaks, or an A/C unit that doesn't work. One of the local storeowners also suggested she negotiate a "rent-free" period to allow her time to build out the property, paint the interior, install fixtures, and generally get the space ready for a grand opening. This will also afford her an opportunity to begin generating revenue before she starts paying rent.

Upon seeing her storefront and "Grand Opening Soon" sign, people start coming out of the woodwork. She makes more new friends who help her understand how to purchase the kinds of clothing lines and accessories she wants to sell. If Camryn wants to design her own clothes someday, she knows she will need to understand apparel design and construction processes, fabric cutting, assembly procedures, trim selection, and finishes. Once she gets her purchasing processes in place, she will have to implement a system to receive it into stock, manage her inventory, and generally merchandise the store. She has her "factory" nearly ready and is prepared to focus on the marketing and sales processes.

Marketing and Sales are all too often overlooked, yet are the lynchpins to success for a small business owner. Now that her store is nearly ready to open, Camryn will need to know how to create awareness and promote her new business, *Chez Camryn!* She doesn't have the resources to afford professionally produced commercials to air on prime-time TV. At least initially, she will do some local marketing that she can manage on a shoestring budget.

Her friends and family help her hand out flyers in the neighborhood, and she makes deals with other local merchants to allow her to place her marketing brochures and business cards in their store in exchange for doing the same for them—i.e., quid pro quo (or "something for something" in Latin).

She wants a spectacular grand opening so she can generate some free publicity. Camryn talks to the local music and dance academy and offers their students a venue to showcase their talent. She makes inquiries with her friends and family and connects with a reporter who works for the local news station. She creates a social media presence and posts updates on her store that is opening soon.

Piecing together fabulous outfits and selling clothes her customers will love should be the easy part. Beautiful clothes are her passion. She decides to have fun with it. Camryn reminds herself she isn't "selling" clothes to people who don't want or need her products. On the contrary, she is helping her customers find the clothes they need for work, a first date, a wedding, or to simply make them feel good. As a local business owner, she makes friends easily and gets involved in the community. Things are coming together, and she really believes success is possible. She has gained the self-confidence she needs to be successful!

Ten years later, she has five locations of *Chez Camryn!* in her area. While she has had her ups and downs and made her share of mistakes—as we all do—she persevered and achieved her dream.

One hard lesson she learned early was she had to have the mindset she wasn't going into business to just pay the rent. Nor was she doing this to please her family, friends, or impress a special someone. From the very beginning, she was contemplating how to open her next store. All along, she was thinking "big" and was willing to stay the course to achieve her dreams.

KEY TAKEAWAYS

As an employee, there will be events and things that affect you that will be completely out of your control. These include economic downturns and whether your employer is profitable and able to stay in business. However, if you do the right things, get your education, and become an expert in your field so your value is high on the open market, you could move up to one of the top spots in your company.

If becoming an entrepreneur is more your style, you should now have a better idea of the many details it takes to work through to open a retail store. For what it's worth, most of the planning that it takes to open a retail business also applies whether you open a consulting firm, online business, or construction company. However, as a business owner, there is no human resources department to punt employee issues to. You are HR. You are everything. Another thing that is different from working for a bigger company is, as an entrepreneur, all of your customers are the boss of you. That said, as an entrepreneur, freelancer, or independent contractor, your possibilities are limitless . . . as is your income potential.

For the rest of this book, however, I will focus on how to succeed as an employee. Entrepreneurship is a topic unto itself. I just wanted to plant the idea seedling in your mind so you'll keep your options open later. It's entirely possible your employer could be acquired by a larger company someday and you get laid off in the process. The Scout Motto "Be Prepared" applies here—be in a state of readiness at all times. As you become an expert in your field, you may come to accept a layoff as a gift and realize it's the right time to strike out on your own or form a company with partners who were laid off with you. Many successful businesses were created that way. For now, though, we'll park entrepreneurship and work on designing a career plan to get you started as an employee.

3 – CREATING YOUR PLAN

*"A good plan today is better than
a perfect plan tomorrow."
– George S. Patton*

In order to get where you want to go, you need to have a plan. Without a plan, your chances of succeeding are Slim and None—and Slim left town. In Chapter 1, you completed the Pros & Cons exercise to uncover your reasons to become successful in life. This exercise was intended to help you determine your *purpose*. In Chapter 2, you got a sense of what it would be like to be an employee versus running your own business. The next chapter will describe many of the career options available to you. For this chapter, let's get you ready to draft the first iteration of your career plan.

There are three things you'll need before you can create your plan: 1) a general idea of what you want to do with your life, 2) an unwavering belief you can achieve your dream, and 3) a willingness to do what is necessary to achieve success. With these key components defined, we can start putting together what is called a "straw-man" plan. In the beginning, it's not going to be perfect, but it is a start. You can refine your career plan as you go through the process of figuring out the specific kind of job or specialty you want to pursue. If you are a perfectionist, take a deep breath in and hold it. You can't possibly know everything yet, so don't let perfect get in the way of good. As you learn and grow, you will start filling in all of the blanks. Getting the perfect design takes time.

While it may seem like a lot of work, this is really the fun part. You get to begin making your dreams come true! But first, let's start by breaking down your big, audacious goal into smaller, digestible chunks. Some of you may be thinking I'm oversimplifying things, and I am. With any big undertaking, the smart approach is to decompose the humongous beast into its component parts to make it more manageable. I will provide examples shortly so we can walk through the process together.

Before we get too far along, I should level-set your expectations. Designing a career plan will take time, introspection, and effort. It's hard. Gurus on competitive theory refer to this as a "barrier to entry." In the real world, barriers to entry mean there are conditions that make it very difficult for new players to enter the market. <u>This is what you want</u>. You want your rivals to run out of steam, lose hope, and tire of all the work and dedication it takes to succeed. You want them to drop out of Navy SEAL school. You want them to quit. But YOU will not. YOU will persevere.

> *"Plan for what is difficult while it is easy;*
> *do what is great while it is small."*
> *– Sun Tzu*

The reason I presented the stories comparing an Employee with an Entrepreneur was to walk you through the kind of thinking and mindset it takes to achieve your goals. Through these examples, you were able to witness two blueprints to work your way through the process—whether that's working in the corporate world or for yourself. What these two stories don't get into are all the challenges Camryn and Barrett faced and how hard it was for them emotionally to persevere.

In Camryn's case, she thought she was going to go out of business at first because she wasn't generating enough cash flow to support herself. Many first-time business owners break-even within the first year but still go under because they don't generate enough income to support themselves. I didn't get into details about how she had to work with the banks and her suppliers to extend her credit. Thankfully, she had supportive parents who let her move back home for about a year until the business started taking off. Once established, her business grew wings, she was able to support herself quite comfortably, and was able to open additional stores.

As for Barrett, he was initially devastated when he got rejection letters from his top two school choices. In retrospect, however, if he had gone to one of his top two choices, he wouldn't have met the great friends who helped him connect with the Le Mans GT pit crew. He could have wallowed in disappointment and given up, but he didn't. When he thinks back to the times he had to miss social events and weekend parties to study, he's glad his dad told him about belated gratification. Yes, he had to forego some fun in the short term, but the payoff for sticking with his plan and not wavering paid off for him big time. He was able to graduate from a great school with honors and get a job offer with the company he wanted.

How Camryn and Barrett achieved their dreams is not a mystery. There are many ways to succeed in your chosen path and it's all there for the taking. To assist you, below are four guidelines you can include into your career design to help you achieve success.

"America is too great for small dreams."
– Ronald Reagan

DREAM BIG

It's okay to dream big. Visualizing what you want can help you define what it is you really desire. In fact, dreams help you develop the desire needed to overcome all the things that can get in your way.

Dreams can turn into passion . . . Passion can turn into plans for action that can change your life. Envision the desired end state— i.e., what success will look like for you. Aim for the stars so that even if you come up short, you will still have gone farther than most others ever dared to dream.

Write your career goals down on paper. Reaffirm your goals often. Every day, you should do something to chip away at the next level of detail that will help you achieve your dreams.

BELIEVE IN YOURSELF

When you are ready to choose a career, make sure it is something you love. Find something that is your passion—something you believe in. Look in the mirror and envision yourself as a great success in that role. If the dream fits you, then you will know it in your heart. You will *feel* good about your choice.

Tell your family, friends, teachers, professors, and counselors about your goals. Once it's out there, you are committed. If you tell others about your career goals, you will be surprised by how many of your sister's friend's cousins know someone in the industry who can help. Networking is a great way to create your own "luck."

Surround yourself with people who support you and who are positive thinkers. Not every day is going to be sunshine and daisies. When you go through a rough patch, your friends and family will be there to pick you up and make you feel better. If you feel stressed, your best friend or sweetheart will say the right things to help you through it. They believe in you for a reason. On the other hand, if you continually hang out with people who have no ambition and no goals, you could find yourself being dragged down. Birds of a feather flock together. It's much better if you choose to socialize with friends who are positive thinkers. It rubs off.

One last thought on the subject . . . When you take on a new task or learn something new, it pushes you out of your current **comfort zone**. Trust in yourself and have the confidence you can do it. Once you complete the task you were initially uncomfortable with, you'll find you've raised your comfort bar to a higher level. That's how you continually grow your skills over time.

THINK IT THROUGH

If you want to do something you've never done before, you'll have to learn how to figure things out. Your inner voice should tell you that you will do *whatever is needed* (that is ethical and legal) to achieve your goal. When I'm faced with a challenge, I start researching to find out who has done this before. I put together a list of things I'll need to do to accomplish the mission, then I reach out to people who are the "experts" who have already solved this riddle before.

Let's use a practical example so we can walk through this together. For our example, assume you want to win the Process Improvement of the Year Award. Your company presents this award every year to the team who implements a process improvement that makes the biggest positive impact on the company. You have six months to prepare. Now what?

To win this award, you'll need to get the support of your team. You'll have to find a way to inspire them to *want* to win and to put in the effort necessary. Your teammates will naturally ask, "What's in it for me?" Always keep that in mind while putting your plan together. Do you have a good relationship with your teammates? Do you know what motivates them to come to work every day? Do you know what their goals are? If not, find out.

When you have a good feel for what your teammates need, you're ready to begin shaping how you are going to secure their buy-in. Put together a proposal that emphasizes how winning the award will help them personally and professionally. Selling points might include a bonus for the team who wins the award, company-wide recognition, and/or virtual poker chips they can use for their next performance review.

Once you have your team's support, talk to your boss. He needs to be on board too. By this time, your sales pitch will include the vital fact the whole team wants to do this. Of course, you can highlight that winning this award will benefit the whole company and, by the way, be a feather in your boss's cap too. Once he's warmed up to the idea, ask for advice on who you should contact to help the team. Get him to confirm his active support so everybody will be driving toward the same goal.

Find out who the judges are and on what criteria they'll base their decision. For this award, you learn entrants must submit a video describing the team, its purpose, what process they've improved, and how it benefited the company. As I've mentioned earlier, you don't want to reinvent the wheel, which is a waste of energy. Instead, find out who the winners were over the past few years. What are the financial benefits of your process improvement? Who needs to be involved in producing the video, and how long will that take? These answers will be integral inputs to your plan.

Now you need to find out what your customers really want from your team. It won't help your cause to put a lot of effort into improving a process you think is important only to find out your customers really don't care about it. A great way to uncover what's important to your customers is to send a survey asking what services they want and what their expectations are. By the way, whoever benefits from the support services you provide are your **customers**.

Armed with survey feedback, assemble the team to interpret your findings and brainstorm for ideas on how to improve service delivery. With this newfound knowledge, you can put together a list of action items and develop an action plan to improve the right process for the right reasons.

MAINTAIN YOUR FOCUS – PERSEVERE

As you execute your career plan, maintain focus on what needs to be done. Don't get sidetracked with things that could lead you off the path. As time goes by, things may change, so be flexible enough to adapt your thinking if new information presents itself. Don't be too rigid in your mindset. Be open to new ideas, and remember, there's always more than one <u>right way</u> to accomplish something.

You will inevitably encounter obstacles you may not have seen coming. Nobody has a crystal ball that foretells the future. Be flexible. Whenever I start planning a new project, I always tell people that I reserve the right to exercise good judgment at any time. This *Get-Out-Of-Jail-Free* card allows you to change your mind if you need to course correct. The path you take to achieve your goals will be fraught with risk, doubt, unfairness, setbacks, and the unknown. Every day, something will test your resolve.

If your mind is made up and you have the will, you may even find you're able to laugh when challenges arise. There is also some level of comfort knowing people with lesser resolve will quit under the same circumstances, but not you. When you falter, pick yourself up, dust yourself off . . . learn from it . . . and continue with the mission.

*No matter how many mistakes you make
or how slow you progress, you're still
way ahead of everyone who isn't trying.*
– Tony Robbins

PLANNING TOOLS

The timelines below represent a couple of different ways to develop your plan to attend a trade school, two-year college, or four-year university. You can adapt this to meet your specific needs.

To develop your timeline (or Gantt chart), draw a horizontal line that represents how long you believe it will take for you to accomplish your goals. (You reserve the right to change things as you work through your plan). List the major things you'll have to do and in what order. Then draw a box to represent that activity. The box should represent approximately how long you think it will take to accomplish that task. This is called **timeboxing**. It doesn't have to be perfect at this point. Life will throw enough surprises your way to alter your plans on the fly. The main thing is to have a plan. If you find you need to revise your plan, then change your plan and work to the new plan. At least you have a plan!

TRADE SCHOOL / COMMUNITY COLLEGE PLAN

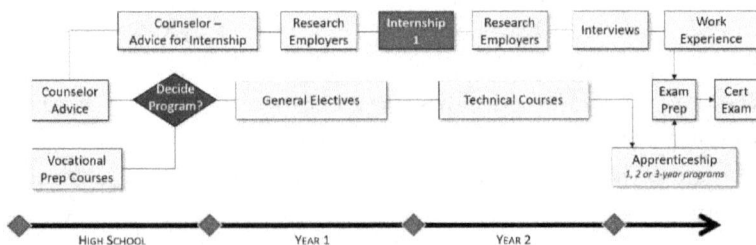

Figure 2: Trade School / Community College Plan

FOUR-YEAR UNIVERSITY PLAN

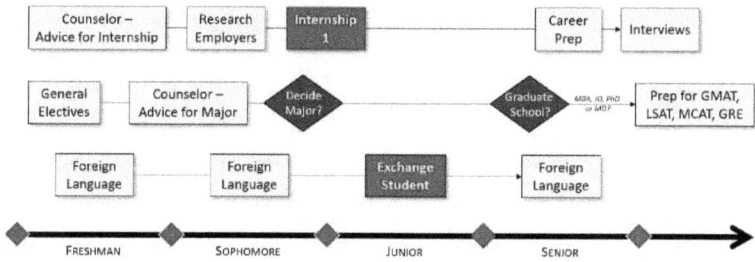

Figure 3: Four-Year University Plan

4 – CAREER OPTIONS

*"You don't have to be a genius or a visionary
or even a college graduate to be successful.
You just need a framework and a dream."*
– Michael Dell

For many years, Detroit, Michigan was known as the automotive capital of the world. The success of the Big 3—General Motors, Ford, and Chrysler—their suppliers, and other manufacturers who were part of the industrial revolution lifted our economy to new heights. In the 1950s, manufacturing essentially created the middle class and helped millions achieve the American dream—i.e., one could achieve success through hard work, initiative, and determination.

With the signing of the NAFTA (North American Free Trade Agreement) on January 1, 1994, politicians promised this deal would increase exports and create thousands of jobs. Instead, American companies were forced to compete globally with third-world and developing countries who paid factory works pennies on the dollar compared with the USA. Heightened competition drove companies to search for ways to lower labor and manufacturing costs. This resulted in industry consolidation and the end of American dominance in the auto industry.

Twenty-five years later, we're experiencing NAFTA's true impact: American jobs were replaced by robotics, automation or relocated overseas. The economy lost much of the manufacturing base that provided many jobs for unskilled labor. Now, those unskilled workers are competing with younger workers for other unskilled jobs, such as those in restaurants, retail, and other service businesses.

Today, with new developments in technology impacting so many parts of our lives, the odds of succeeding are much lower for someone with no skills, no trade, and no education or training to advance from an entry-level position. Corporate America seems to have grown tired of investing in developing its own talent. The scenario where you could graduate with a high-school diploma (or not), get an unskilled job with high pay, and retire with a pension is an era long gone. Likewise, the odds are poor that you will land an entry-level job in the mailroom with a Fortune 500 company and, through hard work and a little luck, move up to the corner office in the executive suite. If your plan is to be hired by your dream company with little to no formal education, training, or skills, then you are misguided. In today's economy, you will be paid what the market will bear . . . and the market is constantly changing.

One of my best friends is among the most honest, hardworking people I know. Throughout his career, he worked long hours and had a passion for excellence. He worked seventeen years for the same manufacturing plant and over the years moved up from Press Operator to Quality Engineer. Then one day, the company was acquired. Less than a year later, the company moved their manufacturing operations out of state and he was out of a job. To make matters worse, he lost his job in Detroit—where manufacturing jobs had been steadily declining for years. This was in 2007 right after the mortgage bubble burst and the economy was on life support. Nobody was hiring and many plants were laying people off, consolidating operations, or going out of business.

Is it fair? There is no such thing as "fair" when it comes to life and your career. When you experience things in life, and the "that isn't fair" thought bubble pops up, be quick to compartmentalize it into a "life isn't fair" bucket and move on. Yes, there are "lucky" people who (by accident of birth) are wealthy, are promoted faster than others, or in your view, get something for nothing. Maybe they earned it. Maybe they didn't. Regardless, it doesn't change your situation. You can't let anything deter you from achieving your goals. Focus on your greatest asset . . . YOU. Your time is better spent paying attention to enhancing your skills, education, and knowledge. You can make no better investment.

Learn the lessons of the past. Learn from people you trust, such as your parents, older siblings, teachers, family members, or friends, who have overcome difficult obstacles and whatever life threw at them and yet still achieved. Don't choose to be a victim. Turn VIC<u>TIM</u> into VIC<u>TORY</u>. Take control of your destiny. This is important for you to understand so you don't allow yourself to be mired in jealousy and envy.

"Life is rough for everyone . . . Life isn't always fair.
Whatever it is that hits the fan, it's never evenly distributed
—some always tend to get more of it than others."
– Ann Landers

EMPLOYMENT REALITIES

I have worked with many people who thought it was the responsibility of their employer to make sure they were promoted, got a big raise, or were assigned the most interesting, fun jobs. It is not. Your employer is in business to make money. That said, smart employers and good bosses create favorable environments for their employees to succeed. Successful companies recognize employees are their greatest asset, and the best ones invest in nice facilities, a break room, a cafeteria, and maybe even a gym. If you are an office worker, your employer will likely provide a laptop, monitors, ergonomic mouse, keyboard, and smartphone. If you work in the field, they may provide you a vehicle, tools, a smartphone, tablet, or a laptop. Why do they do this? So you can be more productive, which in turn, makes them more money.

The good news is there are plenty of different ways to become fulfilled in your career and achieve success. Understand that college is not attainable for everyone. In fact, according to analysts at the

Federal Reserve Bank of New York, roughly 25 percent of those with bachelor's degrees in the US derive no economic benefit from their degree. For that quartile, their pay is equivalent to that of a high-school graduate. On the other hand, there is a 75 percent probability you will do better with a college degree or trade school certificate than someone with only a high-school diploma.

In today's world, employers are more inclusive when it comes to closing the gender gap. Recent statistics revealed close to 60 percent of all college students are women, which helps when it comes to getting higher-paying jobs. Likewise, US Census Bureau data shows more young women are earning college degrees, delaying having children, and choosing to join the workforce. As a result, they are edging out millennial men for better-paying jobs.

Although I can't possibly fit all the different types of jobs in the world in the pages that follow, I have tried to include some of the best-paying jobs that are expected to be in the highest demand in coming years. Not included are more entry-level or low-paying jobs like retail or restaurant jobs, farm workers, and janitors. Unless you are in management, these jobs are not relatively well compensated when compared to the professions described herein.

I hope you find the following sections helpful in raising your awareness about the many career choices available. Trade school vocations are featured first, then you will find the sections evolve into job family groupings where educational requirements are mixed throughout. Feel free to skip to the sections that interest you most.

Trade Schools

You can find trade schools in just about every big city. Also referred to as Technical or Vocational schools, these institutions offer great training opportunities if college isn't for you. The main benefit to attending a trade school is you can get an industry-relevant, focused education that should enable you to get you a job in a related field upon graduation in a shorter period of time than college would.

These schools offer many different fields of study. You can learn the fundamentals for a wide variety of careers such as a Heating, Ventilation, and Air Conditioning (HVAC) technician, electronics tech or electrician, heavy equipment operator, truck driver, auto or marine mechanic, plumber, welder, healthcare, or even the culinary arts.

A good way to find out if one of these vocations is a good fit for you is to visit with a guidance counselor. They have a wealth of information and may even be able to arrange an onsite visit to a local employer who hires workers in a field that interests you. If you can do an onsite visit or a ride-along, you'll get a firsthand look at what a day in the life of your future career might look like.

MECHANICALLY GIFTED

If you are car (or truck) person and like to fix things, you can pursue an automotive technology degree or certificate program. Many opportunities exist for automotive and diesel mechanics. After graduating, you can pursue a job with an automotive dealership, an automaker, or one of their suppliers. One of my good friends is a prototype vehicle technician who works on cars scheduled to go into production in three or four years and he loves it. You can also specialize in working on foreign vehicles—i.e., high-performance sports cars, alternative fuels, electric cars, or other exotic vehicles.

If you like racing, get to know people who race. Perhaps you might consider racing karts or a performance driving school where you can network and make friends with other people who (like you) love auto racing. In fact, most professional racecar drivers started their careers racing karts, and many still drive them between seasons to stay on top of their game. Most people are happy to help someone just starting out. Make the right connections, and you could be on your way to someday being a motorsports technician on race day for NASCAR, IMSA, Tudor United SportsCar Championship, or even Formula 1.

Besides being an automotive mechanic or technician, you can specialize in small engine repair, motorcycles, diesel engines, buses, earth-moving equipment, trains, or even military vehicles like armored personnel carriers and tanks. Just know that you might have to join the Army or Marines if you want to work on military vehicles.

FLYING – FIXED WING & HELICOPTERS

If you are drawn to planes or flying, you can also work as an avionics technician to learn how all the electronics work aboard a fixed-wing aircraft or helicopter. I once talked with an avionics technician who traveled the world working for Bell Helicopter as well as an independent contractor. He told me a college degree isn't necessary to join the military and become a warrant officer to fly helicopters. He said another option is to find a local airport that provides flight school training. By the way, a warrant officer ranks just below the commissioned officers (i.e., lieutenant and above) and higher than noncommissioned officers (e.g., enlisted personnel with a rank of sergeant). While other qualifiers exist, a high-school diploma and being at least eighteen years old are the essential requirements.

I have been fortunate to have gotten a glimpse of another world that exists for those who are not earthbound. A friend of the family got her pilot's license and started working for one of the major airlines. Flying is an occupation where women have been making inroads. For those who fly, their world boils down to those who fly and those who don't. It can be a wonderful life.

Some years ago, I flew on a private jet to visit the Knapheide manufacturing facility in Quincy, Illinois. During the flight, I had the opportunity to speak at length with the pilot. He started out just flying charter flights and then, as the company grew, the number of charter flights increased significantly. He was very friendly and clearly understood the need to provide great customer service. I am sure this came into consideration when Knapheide decided to purchase its own company plane. First, they bought a twin-engine plane . . . then eventually a private jet. Today, he flies all over the country, meets a lot of people, and loves what he does for a living.

Don't forget the support personnel on the ground. It takes a lot of work to keep planes safely in the air. The maintenance requirements are very demanding and aviation maintenance technicians can make a great living. This type of occupation also enables you to travel the world if that is what you want. You can do this as a civilian or you can do your twenty years and "retire" from the military with a pension.

CONSTRUCTION

For those who like construction—residential, industrial, or commercial—then being a carpenter, plumber, HVAC (Heating Ventilation Air Conditioning) technician, elevator technician, mason, or electrician can be a rewarding career. If you like variety or working outside, this could be the life for you. I worked a little residential construction when I was a teenager and found it rewarding to drive by a house that I helped build. Be warned though, most jobs in construction can be very demanding physically.

If you want to get into commercial construction, you can be part of a team that builds skyscrapers, schools, roads, bridges, factories, and other huge projects. You could be a heavy equipment operator and drive a bulldozer, backhoe, dump truck, front-end loader, or crane. These are high paying jobs and always in demand if you are skilled and reliable. You could start out as a general laborer and work your way into learning how to operate heavy equipment on the job, or you can also learn through an apprenticeship (that can take up to three years). The preferred path is to get a high-school diploma, complete heavy equipment training at a trade school, and get your commercial driver's license (CDL). Talk to people who are in the industry to see what schools they recommend. Then check them out. It's not that you don't trust them; it's just that your future is too important to trust to one person's opinion.

Regardless of the vocation, it would behoove you to become familiar with all of the trades and the sequence of how new homes or commercial buildings come together. This could lead to career advancement as a general contractor, construction superintendent, project manager, or even running your own company someday.

One of my wife's best friends married a guy who dropped out of Michigan State University after only one year. He thought college was a waste of his time, and besides, he wanted to start his own construction company. So he did. He worked almost non-stop and eventually grew his company to the point where he was building manufacturing plants for automotive suppliers and the Big Three automakers. To reiterate the point: college isn't for everyone. Ask Bill Gates or Mark Zuckerberg.

UTILITY WORKER

Energy and telephone utilities are not going anywhere soon. Everybody needs electric or gas power, and most people still have landline telephones. Consider also the growing renewables field— i.e., wind power and solar panels. Getting a foot in the door with a local utility doesn't necessarily require specialized training. Utilities usually provide excellent training programs with a special emphasis on safety. Entry-level jobs include being a line worker who repairs damaged power or telephone cables due to inclement weather. (I hope you're not afraid of heights.) You would be amazed at how many people run into utility poles every year, steal copper, or accidentally shoot power lines.

Other jobs include control systems technicians who monitor the power or water system controls, fleet mechanics and technicians, and vegetation management—i.e., the crew who trims trees and other vegetation around telephone/power lines.

While utility maintenance is a relatively high-paying job, it is dangerous. When your power goes out in a thunderstorm, linemen may go up forty to fifty feet in the air in a bucket truck repairing power cables or telephone lines so you can get your lights, TV, or telephone back working. Linemen handle this delicate work wearing thick rubber gloves, rubber sleeves, flame-retardant clothing, ceramic-toed boots, eye protection, a hard hat, and a harness. That said, the view from the top of a bucket truck is uplifting.

Power plant jobs are needed everywhere. However, job projections are falling due to the proliferation of renewable energy sources and distributed generation—i.e., people creating their own power sources through solar panels and wind power cooperatives. The work of power plant operators can be somewhat risky, which contributes to why they earn a relatively high median salary.

HEALTHCARE

For those of you who are nurturing, can handle stress well, and want to help others, a healthcare career may be a good fit for you. In my view, people who work in healthcare are the salt of the earth. It can be wonderfully rewarding. Besides being needed, it is one of the fastest growing sectors in the workforce. If you have the smarts, top grades, and are composed under pressure, then your career options could include a Medical Doctor (MD) or Physician's Assistant (PA). Note that while a PA is a step down from an MD, it only takes twenty-four to twenty-seven months of graduate school beyond a bachelor's degree, whereas an MD requires a four-year undergrad plus four years of medical school plus three to eight years of residency. PA salaries are typically in the six-figure range, and MDs make twice to three times that.

In addition, fields such as nursing are available. Entry-level nurses are called a Certified Nursing Assistant (CNA) and are the first-level support in hospitals. CNAs measure vital signs, perform hygiene for their patients, and help them dress, eat, and use the bathroom. A Licensed Practical Nurse (LPN) monitors patient health and administers basic care. LPNs interview patients, document patient history, take blood pressure, change bandages, and assist RNs.

Registered Nurse (RN) and Nurse Practitioner (NP) round out the nursing profession. RNs represent the biggest healthcare occupation out of them all. RNs take vital signs, administer medications, assist with patient rehab, and follow physician's orders. Nurse Practitioners (NP) are often compared to a PA and are the top level in this field. NPs can diagnose and treat acute illnesses, prescribe medications, and can see patients on their own. At a minimum, becoming an RN requires an associate's degree, but a bachelor of science in nursing (BSN) is preferred. On the other hand, an NP requires at least a master's degree.

A Nurse Anesthetist, which is an advanced practice nurse who administers anesthesia for surgery or other medical procedures, is yet another option . . . but you will likely want your Certified Registered Nurse Anesthetist (CRNA) certification for that one. Other high-demand specialties include, but are not limited to, Dermatologist, Immunologist, Internal Medicine Specialist, Microbiologist, Orthopedic Surgeon, Plastic Surgeon, ENT (Ear, Nose, and Throat Specialist), Psychiatrist, Neurologist, Oncologist, Optometrist, and many more.

NOT A DOCTOR

Not all healthcare jobs require hands-on patient care or require you to perform surgery. Careers in administration, teaching, and other areas don't require eleven to fourteen years in university training to be a doctor. These opportunities include, but are not limited to, a pharmacist, chiropractor, radiation therapist, physical therapist, occupational therapist, nuclear medicine technologist, speech-language pathologist, prosthetic technician, pharmacist, pharmacy technician, dental assistant, dental hygienist, medical billing, dietician, medical records technician, radiologic technologist, EMT (Emergency Medical Technician), and paramedic.

I am the squeamish type, so a career in providing patient healthcare was never for me. However, my mother, two aunts, and a cousin were Registered Nurses, and my uncle was a doctor. Perhaps you have family members or friends you can talk with if you want to learn more about these professions. I have always admired the strength of character health caregivers have.

What a noble profession it is to help others—literally saving lives. As you can see from the list above, plenty of choices are available to research to see what interests you most. Since these jobs are usually in high demand, you can also make a decent life for yourself and your family as well. For those of you who want the flexibility to live anywhere you want, being in the healthcare field can nearly guarantee you will be able to find work. By the way, experienced RNs can get a commission in the military as an officer and, depending upon their qualifications, could join as a Lieutenant, Captain, or even a Major.

Another healthcare option to consider is becoming an Optometrist, which requires only four years of post-graduate coursework. On the other hand, an Ophthalmologist, which is really a medical doctor, requires the eight years of post-graduate work, is licensed to practice medicine, and can perform eye surgery. An optometrist is a person you see when you go to get glasses. No surgery. They perform vision tests, diagnose sight problems (such as nearsightedness or farsightedness), and eye diseases, such as glaucoma. They also prescribe eyeglasses and contact lenses. This is a growing field because of an aging population, and vision problems tend to occur more frequently as people get older. If you want to be an entrepreneur, you can even open your own retail vision store.

Another rewarding, well-paying career with good job security is in the field of Pharmacy. It is important to distinguish between Pharmacists and Pharmacy Technicians. While both jobs dispense medications and deal with insurance companies, physicians, and customers, pharmacy technicians are not allowed to dispense medication without having it reviewed and approved by a pharmacist. Likewise, the education requirements for pharmacy technicians don't require much formal training beyond high school, but pharmacy technicians do have to pass the PTCE (Pharmacy Technician Certification Exam). On the other hand, Pharmacists are required to hold a Doctor of Pharmacy (or PharmD) degree in pharmacology. It is a six-year degree and requires a one-year internship under a licensed pharmacist. After that, you must pass the NAPLEX (North American Pharmacist Licensure Examination) test and register with the Board of Pharmacy in your state. Once registered as a certified pharmacist, you will likely be a top-10-percent earner for the rest of your life.

Before I close out this section, I need to include other fields that offer the highest paying specialties, such as Ultrasound Technician, Radiologic Technologist, Dietitian or Nutritionist, Occupational Therapy Assistant, and Physical Therapist Assistant. Check out your local community college or vocational school for more details.

VETERINARIAN

Let us not forget veterinary medicine. If you love animals, then you may find this rewarding and fulfilling to diagnose, treat, and make animals feel better. According to the American Veterinary Medical Association, there are over 150 million cats, dogs, horses, and other pets in the United States. In addition, the APPA (American Pet Products Association) says that Americans spent more than $50 billion on pets per year in 2014. The demand for pet care is evident, and you can elect to go into mixed animal practice or specialize in only one type of animal, such as equine veterinarians who care for horses. Similar to human healthcare, veterinarian specialties are varied. They include surgery, dentistry, emergency/critical care, and internal medicine. Good vets can make close to six figures or more, and this is a field where owning a pet hospital or clinic is viable.

Art and Design

I didn't include careers such as movie actor or professional musician in this section for the same reason I didn't include professional athletes. For the most part, those occupations don't pay very well unless you're in the top decile of your profession. That said, you can make a good living if you have some artistic skills.

My brother-in-law is a perfect example. He initially went to business school at a major university to get a bachelor's degree in business, because it was the safe, smart thing to do. Yet after working in his field for a year, he realized he couldn't see himself doing this for the rest of his life. He quit his job and went to art school, got his art degree, and is now working in digital advertising . . . and loves it. In fact, in 2017 one of his commercials won an Emmy!

If your family or friends are discouraging you from pursuing your dreams . . . don't listen to them. Perhaps you want to become a sculptor, painter, or design your own line of jewelry. If you believe you have the talent, then follow your heart. However, if an art career is your Plan A, it doesn't hurt to have a Plan B, because if you end up having trouble paying the bills with Plan A, you can make a living with Plan B and satisfy your artist passion doing it as a hobby.

INDUSTRIAL AND PRODUCT DESIGN

An amazingly broad range of choices are available in the field of industrial art and design. Product designers design cars, appliances, toys, electronics, or furniture for a living. Interior design includes residential, commercial, automotive interiors, hotels, and resorts.

Any product on TV, online, or in a store first had to be conceptualized and have drawings created both for product design and manufacturing. Many industries offer a comfortable career as a

CAD (Computer Aided Design) drafting specialist working with engineers to design the tooling to manufacture products or the actual product design itself.

ILLUSTRATION AND GRAPHIC ARTS

It takes a creative, innovative, and talented person to design those captivating print ads in magazines, billboards, and product packaging. Imagine yourself creating multimedia websites, art for marketing layouts, or digital animation for TV commercials. You can get your foot in the door by getting training and/or an internship as a photographer or graphic artist. I know true "artists" may not want to sell out by going "corporate," but marketing and advertising is big business and does pay the bills.

FASHION DESIGNER

The world of fashion design includes more than just designing clothing, shoes, hats, and accessories. You can also specialize in surface design for a wide range of media, including paints, dyes, fibers, yarns, silkscreen, and textiles. Art schools are in many major cities, as well as opportunities to learn online, and offer this specialty. If fashion is your dream, then pursue it.

FINE ARTS

If theater, film, or television is your dream, then be sure to research your options carefully in this very competitive field. Note, however, that actors are just the tip of the iceberg when you consider all the people that support the film industry.

Within the performing arts, Actors make up a small percentage who are involved in making movies or television shows. If you ever have been on the set of a TV show or for a movie, you'll notice camera operators, best boy (lighting technicians), casting coordinators, computer / special effects, costumers (wardrobe), sound technicians, make-up artists, set construction, storyboard artists, video editor, and writers. At the end of a movie, you will see a short list of actors. The rest of the credits are all the others it takes to produce that film. So if you don't necessarily want to act, other opportunities exist to become part of the entertainment industry.

Likewise, there are occupations that don't require you to have Rembrandt-like artistic ability. These jobs require more technical skills. You can work for a museum or art gallery as an administrator, museum curator, art restorer, or archivist. You can also become an art teacher, professor of art history, interior designer, or even cake decorator. These types of careers can allow you to do what you love to pay the bills and make a nice life for yourself and your family.

Business

If you want to be in management, work in Corporate America, or for yourself as an entrepreneur running your own business, then taking classes in or earning a degree in business will help. Careers in business include FAME jobs like Finance, Accountants, Management, and Economics. While there are other specializations, such as organizational behavior, marketing, and sales . . . for the most part, I will focus on the most common professions in business.

ACCOUNTANTS

Whether you run your own business or are working for a small company, mid-sized organization, or multi-national corporation, they all need to keep score on how they are doing financially. **Accountants** record all business and financial transactions as well as report income, liabilities, and assets for an organization. This is used for cash-flow management, banking, taxes, and for reporting performance to stockholders. You will need to be a self-starter and not mind working in small teams or alone. Be aware that accountants are known for having to work long hours during peak business periods, such as tax season or month-end, quarterly, and year-end closing processes.

Top entry-level college graduates may get their first job with a large accounting and consulting firm, where they usually specialize in a specific area such as audit, tax, or real estate. Other accountants may want to work for smaller firms where they get exposure to a wider range of accounting functions. At some point after meeting the minimum work experience requirements, you may want to sit for the CPA (Certified Public Accountant) exam. As a CPA, you are considered a trusted financial adviser. Further, this is not a one-time thing. To retain your CPA certification, you will have to take continuing education courses to maintain your CPA certification.

You can work as an accountant in ANY industry. For example, my cousin earned his bachelor's degree in accounting and immediately applied to the FBI (Federal Bureau of Investigation). He did not get the job during his first attempt because they suggested he get some real-world experience first. He took their advice, worked in the private sector for some years, and applied again. He has been with the FBI his whole career working white-collar crime using his forensic accounting skills. Although sometimes confused with finance analysts, accountants are focused on reporting the historical performance of an organization.

FINANCE

On the other hand, **Finance** professionals, analysts, advisors, and the like are more oriented toward future financial planning, analyzing return on investment for a particular project or program, and predicting the potential for profit or growth of investments for portfolio decision making. Typical jobs for finance majors include financial advisor for an investment company, working as a stockbroker or bond trader on Wall Street, or as a financial management analyst for a company.

Generally speaking, financial advisors provide planning and investment advice to help people save/invest their money for wealth building and retirement. In the corporate world, finance analysts help companies maximize the value of potential investments by calculating which business cases offer the biggest return on capital. Likewise, they monitor and report on the financial health of inflight projects in their investment portfolio. While finance professionals are needed in every industry, they are most commonly associated with working for banks, pension funds, and insurance companies.

MANAGEMENT

General **Management** majors can take courses in accounting, finance, information systems, organizational behavior, marketing, operations management, business strategy, and policy. This provides some flexibility to students who may not be sure what they want to specialize in yet. Likewise, people who take management courses will find it is a great way to develop a broad range of experience sets as well as leadership skills. It is not uncommon for management majors to move up the ranks into executive positions in their careers. For example, some companies identify Hi-Pot (short for High Potential) employees and have them work six months in just about every department of the company before promoting them to a leadership position. If you do well in school and can demonstrate that you have proven leadership qualities by being president of your class, frat, sorority, or other school organization, this may serve you well when corporate recruiters come calling.

ECONOMICS

General Business majors tend to find jobs similar to their concentration in school—i.e., accounting majors work (at least initially) in accounting-related jobs. On the other hand, the field of Economics has a much broader perspective. **Economics** is essentially the study of supply and demand for goods and services, how people use resources and respond to policies, regulations, and other incentives for the greater good. The best economists understand historical trends, the current business climate, and can make accurate predictions.

An economics degree will involve skills in mathematics, statistics, and critical thinking. While you can branch into other fields with an economics degree, if you want to specialize in this field, you will need a post-graduate degree—i.e., at least a master's degree, but a PhD is preferred. Job opportunities include careers in government, banking, investment firms, market research consulting, and of course, college campuses as a professor.

SALES, MARKETING, AND ADVERTISING

If you are the fun-loving, outgoing, energetic, creative type that wants to make a splash in the world, consider a career in **Marketing** or Sales. Marketing involves creative art such as advertising, sales promotion, marketing communications, public relations, market research, consumer behavior, marketing strategy, and sales. Market researchers study consumers and try to understand what they want and what customer experience is through journey mapping. In the real world, they work with social media, product development, big data analytics, professional services, and sales management leaders to develop a marketing strategy to maximize market share and profitability.

Advertising folks create those catchy taglines like 'It's the real thing' (Coke) and eye-catching images and ad copy for print advertising for magazines ads and billboards. They understand how customers think, feel, and react to stimulus. This requires a little bit of psychology, sociology, and public relations skills. They produce commercials that make you feel empathy, make you sad, or make you laugh, and some of the best ones are those great Super Bowl television commercials.

Sales is the profession that drives the economy. In free markets, economies are stagnant until somebody buys something, right? That said, it is a tough profession and requires assertive types with thick skin. On a positive side, sales professionals have nearly unlimited earnings potential. Of course, job security depends on your point of view. If you are great at selling, you will always be in demand. Besides, salespeople are part of a Profit Center—not a Cost Center. They generate revenue for the company, which makes top performers extremely valued. If a company experiences a downturn or an unexpected product recall that causes sales to dip, they are not going to lay off the golden goose. Companies will downsize staff who are considered overhead working in cost centers before cutting their rainmakers.

Salespeople fall into two categories—farmers and hunters. **Farmers** are salespeople who have large, named accounts with a company's most important customers. Job titles vary, but they are usually called account managers, account representatives, or account executives. Their mission is to grow revenue. They accomplish this by building strong partnerships with their clients, becoming industry experts, and offering solutions to problems their customers have.

Another similar role, yet distinct to the farmer, is the inside salesperson. The type you are likely most familiar with are sales clerks who help you when you shop at a retail store. Inside sales professionals (or telemarketers) also make outbound or take inbound calls when you want to buy something over the phone. For inside sales, customers essentially seek them out. On the other hand, telemarketers are normally part of high-volume call centers and make their living on the phone.

Hunters are the most assertive types of salespeople. They are ambitious and highly motivated to succeed. In the words of a good friend, hunters are *coin-operated*. The most successful ones know how to prospect for leads and are skilled at asking questions to determine prospective clients' business needs, challenges, or pain points. As a subject matter expert, they have enough product depth and industry knowledge to offer innovative solutions to customer problems. The best sales pros are rewarded for their efforts. In fact, SALES is easily the highest-paid profession (except for professional athletes and actors). That's right. Top sales professionals make more than doctors, dentists, lawyers, and pilots.

Qualifications needed for the successful career in sales include, but are not limited to, having self-confidence, being a great listener, and possessing the ability to quickly build rapport with others. If this is a profession you want to pursue, your personality traits and qualifications should include being a skilled communicator, ultra-competitive, organized, and persistent. Compensation for high-end sales professionals customarily consists of a base salary plus a commission for the deals they close. Other perks may include company cars, vacations, trips to resorts for "conferences," stock options, bonuses, etc. It is a high-risk, high-stress, high-reward profession.

COMMUNICATIONS AND PUBLIC RELATIONS

If you are a great communicator and want to do something that leverages those skills, without the added pressure of trying to sell a product or a service, then **Public Relations** (PR) or **Corporate Communications** may be for you. Nearly all mid-sized to large companies and many governmental institutions have public relations (or public affairs) departments. The larger an organization is, the more likely it needs dedicated staff to manage internal and external relationships among its employees, government, industry organizations, and the press. Together, the corporate communications and PR departments are responsible for managing an organization's reputation.

While public affairs officers focus on relationships external to the organization, the scope of **Corporate Communications** is usually a mix of external and internal. The mission is to influence, entertain, and inform others. Communications professionals use a mix of media delivery channels best suited to communicate their message to their target audience. This includes communicating in person and using print, social media, and/or television. Other duties include event planning, working with marketing and advertising, and developing publicity campaigns to get the word out on what current projects or initiatives with which the organization is involved.

In many ways, the corporate communications team mission is very similar to marketing and advertising in the sense they both function as a spokesperson and point of contact for media relations. Instead of trying to sell goods or services, their goal is to maintain good relations with industry, government, and the media. In short, they sell ideas, policies, and try to promote goodwill for the organization.

Publicity is also measurable. Since for-profit organizations are in business to make money, communications professionals have developed a way to quantify the benefit and effectiveness of a particular campaign. For example, if the company CEO interviews with a national cable news reporter about a new product rollout and gets high primetime ratings, communications specialists can convert the value the goodwill it created using the Advertising Cost

Equivalent (ACE), which is the measure of what you would have had to pay for the equivalent advertising space.

If you want to develop your skills as an expert public speaker and be at the forefront of communications using social/print/digital media channels, this choice could be a great match.

STEM (Science, Technology, Engineering, & Mathematics)

As our world becomes more digitalized and technology integrates into every facet of our lives, STEM occupations will be the highest demand occupations needed in the future. With exceptions for doctors, lawyers, and top salespeople, STEM occupations typically offer higher salaries than non-STEM jobs. According to the US Department of Commerce, STEM occupations are growing at 17 percent, while other occupations are growing at 9.8 percent.

You will note the sections that follow are a bit out of sequence with STEM. This is because I wanted to focus on the high-demand occupations within Science, Engineering, and Technology first. Also, I won't address Mathematics in detail since, in my opinion, all STEM occupations require higher-level math skills anyway. Besides, other than teaching and research, the primary fields of Mathematics are limited to statistics, actuarial science, and to some extent, cryptography.

SCIENCE

Careers in Science can be broken down into Earth and Environmental Science, Physical and Life Science, and Behavioral Science. Careers in high demand for Earth and Environmental Science include fields such as Geography, Surveying, and Cartography. **Geographers** study the earth and the distribution of its land, features, and inhabitants. A **Cartographer** is a person who creates maps, whether they are of the world, roads, train routes, or archeological sites. **Surveyors** make precise measurements to determine locations or property boundaries. They also provide information regarding the shape and contour of the earth's surface for mapmaking, construction, and civil engineering projects.

For all these fields, the ability to work with data has become increasingly important, and they incorporate technologies such as Global Positioning Systems (GPS) and Geographic Information Systems (GIS). Most people are familiar with GPS since it helps in finding devices and locations. An example is in your smartphone, which uses a vast network of satellites located in space that locate specific coordinates on the earth's surface. Originally developed by the US military in the 1960s, GPS technology is used in the automotive industry for applications such as having a hidden GPS transmitter to keep track of the location of your car in case it's stolen so police can recover it and/or catch the thief. In addition, GIS technology is the main part of what enables driverless and self-driving vehicles.

High-demand jobs in Physical Science that require a PhD include Physicist, Astronomer, Biochemist, Materials Scientist, or Chemist. These fields are essentially all research scientists. You will spend most of your time in a lab environment conducting experiments, analyzing statistical data, and writing papers to report your findings. It's rewarding work for those of you who have strong mathematics abilities, complex reasoning skills, critical thinking, and the ability to focus on solving a problem for extended periods of time. If that sounds like your cup of tea, the fields below offer a glimpse of what you can be.

Physics is the science concerned with the nature and properties of matter, energy, and time. **Physicists** perform theoretical research to try to understand how the universe was created and how it is changing, while others try to develop alternate sources of energy or ways of treating cancer through radiotherapy and diagnosing illness through various types of imaging—e.g., x-ray, CT scan (also called CAT scan, short for Computed Tomography Scan), MRI (Magnetic Resonance Imaging), ultrasound, nuclear medicine imaging, etc.

Astronomers study our universe, such as our sun, stars, planets, solar systems, galaxies, and black holes. Much like Physicists, Astronomers are trying to learn how the universe works using telescopes, ground-based equipment, and space-based systems like satellites and the Hubble Space Telescope. If this is an area of interest, take a look at the NASA (National Aeronautics and Space Administration) website. There, you can learn all about the latest launch schedule and missions by visiting NASA Missions A-Z. In addition to the International Space Station, they are working on the Hubble Space Telescope, Mars Rover, Juno Mission to Jupiter, and New Horizons: Pluto and Beyond, among scores of others. NASA is always looking for research scientists and engineers with specializations in aerospace, aviation, biology, physics, electrical, mechanical, and others.

Biochemists are research scientists who study the chemical and physical properties of organisms to learn about important biological processes. It is primarily laboratory-based research, and some specializations focus on learning how genes mutate and how evolution works. You can also specialize in Genetics, which is a field of biology that studies genes, heredity, and genetic variation. A Geneticist studies genes, including how they are inherited, mutated, activated, or inactivated . . . and the role genes play in disease, such as cancer. Perhaps a geneticist will one day find a gene therapy to cure cancer and help us all live a longer, healthier life.

A **Chemist** is a scientist that researches the properties of chemical substances. They measure the effects of compounds and study chemical reactions. Chemical research has led to the development of new synthetic plastics, nylons, paints, lubricants, and a myriad of products. Material Scientists conduct research to devise ways of improving materials or creating new ways to combine substances for practical use. Unlike Chemists, Material Scientists typically strive to improve existing materials, processes, or products.

ENGINEERING

In my view, the engineering specialties that combine the best value, top pay, most job security, and highest demand are Petroleum Engineers, Aerospace Engineers, Electrical Engineers, Mechanical Engineers, Civil Engineers, and Robotics Engineers. A four-year bachelor's degree in your engineering specialty is required.

If you are into the future of energy, then **Petroleum Engineering** may be for you. My neighbor, who is a research scientist with a Ph.D. Mechanical Engineering, says gasoline is the perfect fuel—much more efficient than alternative energy sources so far. You will find the largest employers of petroleum engineers are in the oil and gas industry. Petroleum engineers design and oversee the prospecting, production, and methods for retrieving oil and natural gas from beneath the earth's surface or via deep sea drilling. In addition, petroleum engineers design, maintain, and build oil pipelines and oil storage facilities.

If you love flying, want to be a pilot, or design aircraft, spacecraft, missiles, or satellites, you should seriously consider becoming an **Aerospace Engineer**. Earth-bound options include working for commercial airlines or joining the military. If exploring space is your goal, then your options are limited in the private sector to working for SpaceX in California, which was founded with the goal of reducing the cost of space transportation. Today, Aerospace Engineers deliver satellites into Earth's orbit as well as cargo and people. Otherwise, you can join NASA (National Aeronautics and Space Administration), which is an independent agency of the United States Federal Government. If you pursue a career with NASA, your mission will be to pioneer the future of space exploration, scientific discovery, and aeronautics research. Existing missions include the International Space Station, Deep Impact (mission to a comet), Mars Rover, Juno mission to Jupiter, and New Horizons mission to Pluto and Beyond. By the way, some NASA satellite missions work with partners such as Boeing and SpaceX.

The field of **Electrical Engineering** (EE) presents a wide range of opportunities because everything that uses electricity must be designed, engineered, and produced. Think of vehicles as computer systems on mechanical platforms where the electronics and wire harnesses are its nervous system. While some fields of electrical engineering do focus on research, the majority of specialties are product development and manufacturing related. Electrical Engineers work with a large variety of products and systems in areas such as aerospace, transportation, power generation, battery/energy storage, manufacturing, industrial controls, and lighting, among others.

My personal favorite engineering specialty is **Mechanical Engineering** (ME). In my experience in the auto industry, Mechanical Engineers are involved with concept design, product design, and packaging (using Computer Aided Design or "CAD" tools), testing, and manufacturing—i.e., art to part. In short, you can design, engineer, and produce nearly anything with an ME degree, including cars, trucks, sport utility vehicles, trains, planes, children's toys, aircraft carriers, wind turbines, manufacturing plants, and all the tooling on the plant. In fact, the dad of one of my best friends started a company that used Engineering Mechanics concepts to develop software that simulated real-world crash testing, material stress / fatigue / failure caused from the effects of external forces, pressures, or thermal characteristics. MEs work in product engineering or manufacturing and are considered the general practitioners of the engineering profession since they work in such a broad range of disciplines.

Civil Engineers plan, design, and manage construction projects that are usually very large in scale. In the private sector, civil engineers work with architects and city planners on projects like office buildings and planning community development. In the public sector, civil engineers are challenged with working on big infrastructure projects, such as roads, tunnels, bridges, railways, subways, airports, dams, floodways, energy and water supply, and waste treatment plants. Employment of civil engineers is projected to grow 20 percent by 2022, which is much faster than the average.

Robotics Engineering is a unique area of specialty. Due to the complexity of creating a human-like system, robotics requires a variety of skills in several fields—e.g., software engineering, electro-mechanical engineering, vision systems engineering, computer engineering, and artificial intelligence. Do we need to worry that robots will replace humans in the workforce? I don't believe we have to worry about that or a Skynet type of threat in this century. Besides, advancements in robotics technologies to date have been focused on developing machines and automation that can substitute for humans and replicate human actions that are repeatable tasks (such as manufacturing) or used in dangerous environments—e.g., firefighting, bomb disposal, and space exploration.

That said, some robots are capable of running like a person, preparing meals, and cleaning a house. Self-driving cars and trucks currently exist on our streets and highways. In addition, prosthetics developed today function essentially as bionic arms driven by brain waves. Someday, we may be able to provide our injured military and civilian citizens replacement limbs so they can continue living a normal life. What an exciting field of engineering to be a part of!

Information Technology (IT)

If you like computers, then a career in Information Technology or "IT" is and will be constantly in demand for the foreseeable future. IT is also referred to as IS (Information Systems), Management Information Systems (MIS), and other names. While you can enroll in a trade school for computer science or network technology, getting a bachelor's degree in Computer Science or equivalent will enable you to go further, at least initially.

Most who enter this field start out in an entry-level position such as a service desk analyst, desktop technician, data center coordinator, or in software quality assurance and testing. Regardless, I recommend you also pursue certification in the field of your choice. In the IT field, certifications or "certs" lend credibility and are oftentimes a mandatory qualification. Most of the top performers do have some formal education and most have professional certifications. To get and stay ahead, you will need to be in continual learning mode. At worst, know that certifications can be tiebreakers when recruiters review your resume.

Career paths in IT are evolving, but essentially, you have three career path choices: 1) technical Subject Matter Expert (SME) or "techy" for short, 2) manager or supervisor in charge of people, and 3) project management or business analyst. By the way, did I mention that the average IT professional is in the top 10 percent of wage earners?

The first category means you are primarily an individual contributor—i.e., programmer, developer, engineer, architect, administrator, analyst, technician, etc. These roles are ideally suited for people who want to become technical experts without having to be responsible for other people. (Not everybody wants to be a manager.)

The second category is for those who want to lead/manage people and teams to accomplish organizational goals. Management titles include supervisor, manager, senior manager, and director. These IT leaders excel at creating collaborative environments, building teams, and delivering solutions via efficient business processes.

The third category is being a project manager, which is kind of like being a manager but without the authority that you have if you are the boss of the people on the project team. Project team members usually report to other resource managers, so a project manager usually doesn't have the power to hire/fire. Hence, diplomacy is a valued skill.

Included in this final category is the business analyst, or what's more commonly referred to as a BA. I often think of BAs as liaisons between the business people and the techies. Good BAs can elicit non-technical business requirements and translate them into pseudo-techy language (read: geek-speak) that techies can understand. This requires a rare mix of skills that include business acumen, technical know-how, organizational skills, communication skills, and the ability to quickly gain the trust of others.

To further classify the types of IT career choices available to you, I divided them into separate domains: IT Service Management, Application Development, Data Science, Cybersecurity, Infrastructure, and Project Management.

IT Service Management

Back in the late 1980s and early 1990s, when IT was relatively new, technical support practices were immature at best. Today, it's much different. Technical support has become fairly sophisticated in terms of the service operation's processes and tools, and it has become a well-respected profession. Internal customer satisfaction is driven by a person's first interaction with the IT department, and 80 percent of the time, that is based on their experience dealing with the Service Desk (a.k.a. Help Desk).

If you have taken computers in high school, trade school, or community college, you can qualify for an entry-level position at a service desk. As I mentioned earlier, this is a great way to get your foot in the door. Most people start out as an Analyst taking technical support calls. While working in the service desk, you can get exposure to a wide range of technologies, such as password resets, desktop technology, telecom, mobile devices, data management, software applications, system integration, servers, storage, and networks. Specialties within the service desk include support center analyst, desktop support technician, quality assurance, and knowledge-centered support analyst, among others.

APPLICATION DEVELOPMENT

This role primarily consists of customer-facing technologies, with roles that include web design, software programmer, application developer or application support analysts. These roles primarily deal with programming code with which end users interact. Unlike the old days where programmers were writing bits and bytes, many of the tools that developers use now automate a lot of the grunt work. Other occupations that help pull together successful applications are graphic artists (if you love art), computer animation (for gamers), and illustrators.

Human-Computer Interaction or "Usability" is a fascinating field too. Usability experts understand how people interact with computers. They focus on helping computer designers build User Interfaces (UI) that are easy to use, easy to learn, efficient, and recoverable when a mistake is made. This is very important in web design because most users have very little patience when using online web sites and mobile apps, so page loading speeds need to be fast. Systems are becoming more powerful and faster every day, and people lose interest if an app is too slow. The target search response time for one of the major search engines is a mere 400 milliseconds (ms), so if you pursue this field, make sure the performance of your code is super-fast.

You can also specialize in database design, development, or administration, and this is a high-demand field. Quality Assurance (QA) professionals perform testing and validation of software; many application developers start out in QA. Application developers (a.k.a. programmer analysts) write the code. Like most occupations in IT, good ones can earn a very nice living. The end product is the software or applications that people or machines use to do their job. Software basically performs calculations or processes that transform and/or store data. If you like creating new solutions to business problems, then being a developer may be for you. By the way, the average application developer's earnings put them in the top 5 percent of wage earners in the USA.

DATA SCIENCE / ANALYTICS / BIG DATA

In its early days, this was often referred to as data mining, report writing, and/or business intelligence. With the explosion of big data, the main opportunities today are as data scientists, big data specialists, and data analysts. Data is embedded into every interaction between humans or machines—it is everywhere. With the IoT (Internet of Things) the amount of data is exploding. With the IoT, we will move toward connecting any device to the Internet, to other devices, to cloud based applications, and to data lakes (i.e., repositories of data stored in their natural format).

In addition to machine learning and artificial intelligence at the endpoints, business and competition are evolving customer experience to be more personalized, which is changing the way we work and live. To consumers, IoT means smart homes that connect smartphones, home security systems, coffee makers, refrigerators, washing machines, thermostats, lighting, and almost anything else. I have read accounts claiming data is growing so rapidly it is doubling every two years. So if you like working with or analyzing data and figuring out ways to slice and dice it and make it valuable to end users, then start researching open source data analytics platforms.

CYBERSECURITY

For those of you who think it would be nifty to protect computer systems and IoT, then Cybersecurity may be a field for you. With the proliferation of technology comes the need to protect it from the bad guys. Hence, Cybersecurity or Information Security (InfoSec) professionals are in high demand because of the growing threat to America—both in the private and public sectors. In the US, we are bombarded by millions of cyberattacks per day and growing— mostly from sources outside the United States. If you perform an online search, look up the keywords "real time cyberattack map," and you'll be astonished by how prevalent cyberattacks are. It's the new battleground frontier.

Malware, email phishing, and ransomware remain some of the most prevalent forms of cyberattacks, and social engineering is still the most vulnerable vector. According to CSO online, 92 percent of malware is delivered by email. When you consider the average cost of a single attack to American companies is in the $5 million range, it's no wonder businesses are scrambling to protect their data and IT assets.

You can research which security certifications are the most sought after. As of this writing, the most recognized international professional association for security training and certification is ISACA (Information Systems Audit and Control Association). At ISACA, you can earn a CISSP (Certified Information Systems Security Professional) certification, which is well respected and generally recognized as the most prestigious in the field. Other certifications include the Certified Ethical Hacker (CEH) credential and CompTIA Security+ certification. Be advised that, in addition to educational qualifications, there is usually mandatory experience required to become an InfoSec professional.

INFRASTRUCTURE

Unlike software development, IT Infrastructure is more of a behind-the-scenes field and contains several specialties. The most prevalent fields are categorized as Compute, Storage, Network, Telephony, and Telecommunications. Compute includes virtualization management and operating systems that are managed by a Systems Administrator, who configures and maintains the server. Storage administrators oversee the vast amounts of data processed in the infrastructure environment and are responsible for backup and recovery of data. With the explosion of data analytics and "big data" mentioned above, these jobs remain in high demand.

As in the mainframe days of the 1980s, Converged Infrastructure (CI) is a popular technology. CI combines virtualization, compute, storage, and the network into one cabinet and is akin to buying a data center in a box. To pursue a job where you can touch all facets of infrastructure, find a company who has invested in CI or Hyper-Converged Infrastructure (HCI). Regardless, there are plenty of opportunities to pursue a career as a Systems Administrator responsible for configuration, maintenance, and troubleshooting for servers and storage systems.

If you would like work in digital "plumbing"—i.e., the way IT systems communicate with each other—then a networking career may be for you. Network administration jobs include things like design, installation, and maintenance of firewalls, network security, and communications protocols. All data, voice, and video must travel from point A to point B somehow—whether the communication is wired or wireless networks. You can research this field, but as of this writing, Cisco, Brocade, and Juniper are the market leaders in enterprise networking. Cisco is the dominant vendor in the US, so I recommend you pursue certifications, beginning with the CCNA (Cisco Certified Network Analyst). Certification tracks are constantly changing, so check with your boss, professor, or Cisco account rep on what best fits your goals and your company's objectives.

Remember, not everyone starts at the top. Even if you must start out with a hands-on job racking and stacking and cabling within the data center, you will have gotten your foot in the door. If you stick with it, the payoff will be there in the long run.

Project Management

A "project" is defined as a planned (usually temporary) set of interrelated tasks to be executed over a fixed period using specific resources within certain cost and other limitations to produce an agreed upon set of deliverables with a defined start and end date. Project management is the process and activity of planning, organizing, and controlling project teams, technical Subject Matter Experts (SME), and vendors to achieve a specific scope of work. Accordingly, Project Managers (PMs) have a broader base of expertise than most other fields.

Project managers are needed for construction, engineering, shipbuilding, business initiatives, and many other endeavors, including IT. Any initiative should be managed as a project if it has a defined scope, must be well planned, has stakeholders who are impacted across multiple departments, and has a specific due date. If you want to excel as a project manager, I recommend you first gain some experience as a technical specialist in any of the aforementioned IT domains first . . . or as a business analyst.

Becoming a Business Analyst (BA) can be a very rewarding job. As I mentioned previously, BAs function as a liaison and translator between the business side of an organization and the technology side. They work with business users to understand the business problem they're trying to solve. When considering career choices, project managers are usually more experienced with higher earnings potential, but top business analysts are not very far behind. The best ones are in the top decile in earnings.

PARALEGAL

Behind every great lawyer is a great paralegal. Ask most lawyers, and they will agree on how indispensable their paralegals are. They help lawyers behind the scenes in nearly every facet of the legal profession. Also referred to as legal assistants, paralegals perform many tasks under attorney supervision, such as researching, drafting letters, and writing or revising provisions within a contract. It also includes investigation, case management, and preparation for and assisting at trial. If you like research and unearthing cases that help your team win a case, this field could be for you. You can earn a certificate at a trade school or take an entry-level position and learn via On-the-Job Training (OJT).

Military Service

Some people worry that the American dream is no longer alive. In fact, a poll conducted by the *Public Religion Research Institute* reveals that 55 percent of Americans say the American Dream either never existed in the first place or that it did exist but doesn't anymore. That is simply not true. Nowhere else in the world can someone rise from having nothing and become successful. In my experience, the military is the great equalizer when it comes to opportunity. Regardless of race or gender, anyone from any part of the country can get ahead.

After twenty years, you are eligible to "retire" from the military with a pension. However, your career isn't over after military service. Examples of ex-military who have achieved über success include: Sperry Shoes, founded by Navy veteran Paul A. Sperry; FedEx, founded by Marine Corps veteran Fred Smith; Walmart, cofounded by Army veteran Sam Walton; and USAA, founded by a group of Army officers. Even if you aren't the next Sam Walton, you can make a nice living in the military by doing a stint in the military as your first career and using it to launch your next one.

ARMY, NAVY, AIR FORCE, MARINES, OR COAST GUARD

One way to get your life straightened out is to enlist in the military. (I did.) As a member of the military, you are part of a group whose common mission is to protect America. I have not found another organization of which I have been prouder to be a member. In addition to all the benefits in the military, you'll make friends for life. Once you are in the military, you can make the choice whether to make it a career or not. Similar to civilian career choices, there are hundreds of different Military Occupational Specialties (MOS) to choose from, so don't think your choices a limited.

For example, if you want to be police officer, detective, DHS, FBI, or CIA agent, then you can pursue an MOS in security services, such as Military Police (MP) or Military Intelligence in any branch of the service. For construction or utility careers, the Army or Marines is the spot to pursue an MOS in combat engineering where you can learn how to be an electrician, carpenter, mason, plumber, or power distribution specialist. If you want to be an air traffic controller, avionics tech, work in public affairs, be a paralegal, become a photojournalist, or learn electronics . . . then the Navy or Air Force may be for you. In all branches, opportunities abound in healthcare for dentists, nurses, and doctors, as well as all the IT fields. Of course, if you are more interested in being a warrior/hero, then Special Forces units like Army Green Beret, Rangers, Navy Seals, or Marine Force Recon are options.

If you are into computers, consider the Air Force or Navy. In my career, many of the best IT people have Navy or Air Force backgrounds. If you re-enlist, you may get a bonus and can retire after only twenty years! If that seems way too far in the future for you to even comprehend, think about this: if you enlist at eighteen you could retire at thirty-eight years old and receive 50 percent of your final salary in pension benefits for the rest of your life. I have worked with ex-military people who have started their "second career" while collecting a military pension! If you are fortunate enough to get a pension from your employer in your second career, having two pensions isn't a bad option for retirement.

In addition to being a warrant officer or non-commissioned officer, you can also become an officer. Military officers are the private sector equivalent of an executive, manager, or supervisor over enlisted personnel. You can become an officer by joining the ROTC (Reserve Officer Training Corps) at a participating four-year university. However, college is not free if you are accepted into an ROTC program. Cadet benefits include scholarships (for eligible students) to assist in covering the costs for tuition, books, and fees, plus a monthly stipend. After graduation, there is an eight-year military commitment, of which three years (or four years for scholarship winners) are active duty, and the remaining years are as a reservist.

While highly selective, if you are a good student and have a solid ACT or SAT score, then one of the military academies may be a fit. If this is a consideration, be prepared for a very structured, challenging environment with rigid rules, but you will also find it to be a proud and rewarding career. Cadets develop strong leadership skills and create lifelong bonds. Plus, you become part of a great American tradition. Career choices are expansive; the range of academic majors offered is very similar to that of public universities. There are five military academies:

1. United States Military Academy, West Point, New York
2. United States Naval Academy, Annapolis, Maryland
3. United States Air Force Academy, Colorado Springs, Colorado
4. United States Coast Guard Academy, New London, Connecticut
5. United States Merchant Marine Academy, Kings Point, New York

The benefits of attending a military academy include zero cost to attend, a great reputation academically, and a guaranteed job as an officer. There is a five-year active duty commitment and three years of reserve duty after graduation. Otherwise, if you would rather join the military part-time you can check out the National Guard or Reserves where you can serve one weekend a month and two weeks a year. Your overall commitment is eight years.

The first step towards getting somewhere
is to decide that you are not going to stay where you are."
– J.P. Morgan

DECIDING ON A CAREER

The career choices above are only a representative sampling of what is available to you. If you are undecided on your future or still have no idea where to start, talk to your school counselor, teacher, recruiter, family, and friends. Likewise, you can search the Internet to drill deeper into career specialties, or you can visit your local library. An abundance of free information awaits to help determine your career. There are also plenty of online tools to help assess your psychological preferences and recommend career fields that fit your personality type. The trick is to be honest with yourself when responding to these assessments.

I need to add a word of caution regarding personality tests. Years ago, I took a new job where I was inheriting a department with over one hundred employees. In an effort to build camaraderie and improve teamwork, I asked my human resources business partner to administer two different types of personality tests—a Myers-Briggs Temperament Sorter and a DiSC Profile Test. Both are great tests, and the results are amazingly accurate.

After everyone took the tests, we all met to share the results together. I was pleased to see how much it helped us recognize how all of us had different interests, beliefs, and values, and the facilitator offered recommendations on how we could work better together. The results also dispelled the notion that IT professionals are all highly analytical, introverted nerds with poor social skills. That's simply not the case. Our personality type results were all over the board. You might think people who had the same jobs would be classified within a narrow band of personality types, but we didn't. And I think that's a good thing! I believe it's better to have different types of people doing the same kind of job so you can benefit from diverse perspectives and different approaches to solving problems.

So be forewarned. If you take some of these strengths-finder, personality, or temperament-sorter tests, don't pigeonhole yourself into thinking you'll only be a fit for the career fields listed within their personality types. Everyone possesses a range of behaviors that are part of other personality types. When it comes to doing what you love, follow your passion and follow your heart. Job satisfaction is all about how it makes you *feel*.

If you are still having difficulty deciding, you can narrow your career choices down by using a **Decision Tree**, which is similar to March Madness brackets. It's easy to use, and you can get results pretty quickly. See the figure below. Start by putting your top choice in the #1 seed, your second choice in the #2 seed, and so on. Put the winner between #1 and #8 in the Semifinal bracket, and continue doing the same thing with the rest of the pairings. As you work through your brackets, envision yourself in the role and what your life would be like before you select bracket finalists. Using this method, you can shortlist your favorites down to a final four . . . or even pick a winner!

DECISION TREE PLANNING TOOL

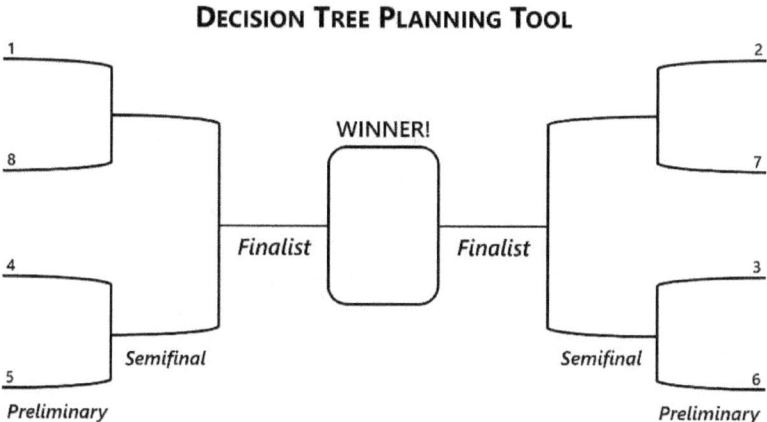

Figure 4: Decision Tree

If at this point you still can't decide, I have provided another decision tool at your disposal. If you can get it down to no more than three or four choices, you're ready for a **Pugh Decision Matrix**. This scientific approach allows you to list your decision criteria, add weight to what is most important to you, and compare calculated scores. It's best to rate them horizontally (by row) for each criterion so you are comparing each one relative to the other. If you find yourself wanting to massage the weighting until you get the results you want, that's okay. That's part of the process.

Career Choice →		Engineer		Technician		Designer	
Criteria	Weight	Raw Score 1	Weight Score 1	Raw Score 2	Weight Score 2	Raw Score 3	Weight Score 3
Allows me to be creative	30%	3	0.90	2	0.60	4	1.20
Able to write/ research	25%	2	0.50	1	0.25	4	1.00
Get to work as part a team	15%	4	0.60	4	0.60	2	0.30
Requires analytical skills	10%	4	0.40	3	0.30	2	0.20
Lots of travel to see the world	15%	3	0.45	1	0.15	2	0.30
High pay, perks, or bonuses	5%	4	0.20	2	0.10	3	0.15
TOTALS	100%		3.05		2.00		3.15

Score by Row, 1 through 4, where 4 is high

Figure 5: Pugh Decision Matrix

If you're still undecided but have narrowed your career choices down to no more than two options, you can use one of the most scientifically advanced methods to determine your preference—the **Coin Flip**. The instructions are easy. Designate *Choice-1* to be HEADS and *Choice-2* to be TAILS. Flip a coin, and let it land on the ground. If the coin comes up heads and you're happy, you're done! However, if it comes up heads and you find yourself wanting to go two-out-of-three, then tails was really your preference all along! Pretty sophisticated, eh?

Figure 6: The Heads-or-Tails Method

All kidding aside, after reading this chapter, you should realize that getting a college degree isn't the only way to become successful. For now, let's assume you have successfully used the tools above to figure out your career choice and are near completion of your education or training program. Now, let's find a job!

Finding a Job

5 – Targeting Your Desired Job

*"A smart man makes a mistake, learns from it,
and never makes that mistake again. But a wise man
finds a smart man and learns from him how to
avoid the mistake altogether."*
– Roy H. Williams

The purpose of this section is to help you find the type of organization you want to work at. I also cover how to prepare a winning resume that is tailored to the position to which you're applying. In addition, I'll provide pointers on the most important things to consider while researching potential employers.

You may have heard the saying: "Measure twice, cut once." It applies here as well. What you do for your career will be your livelihood, so approach the process thoughtfully. For the job hunt itself, you can find plenty of resources outside of this book for that. My goal for this chapter is a little different. I want to share insight and the benefits of gaining experience as an employee first—regardless of whether you decide to make it a lifelong career or use it as a stepping stone to open your own business. In the sections that follow, I explain what to look for when researching the type of company you want to work for. I also provide a sneak peek at what it's like to work for a large company versus a smaller company (or a startup). I recommend you give yourself several months' lead time to start your job search prior to graduating whatever program you are in. You'll greatly benefit from being prepared.

RESEARCHING YOUR TARGET COMPANY

Perhaps you already have a specific company in mind. That's great. Let's call it "Plan A." However, even though you may have your mind set on your target company, it is still pragmatic to have a Plan B, Plan C, or even a Plan D—just in case Plan A does not come through. Business conditions can change quickly. For example, you might want to work for ACME Deep Sea Drilling, but if it is a public company in the midst of a downturn due to falling oil prices, through no fault of your own, they could be laying off people—not hiring. Likewise, if your Plan A is a high-tech company, by the time you graduate, it might be acquired by one of the tech giants with its new headquarters located overseas. Hence, I recommend you develop your plan that goes from general to specific—i.e., start with the industry you want to be in, then the type/size of the company, location, what you want your role to be, etc.

Even if you are an aspiring entrepreneur who plans to open your own business someday, why not pursue a paid apprenticeship? There is nothing wrong with working for another company in your target industry to learn the ropes. Once you're in the game, you will get to work with experts who have already successfully figured out how to run a company in the industry that you want to be in. Why not learn everything you can about the competition, suppliers, customers, and the market leaders' strengths and weakness?

As an insider, you have the luxury of taking this time to figure out a competitive advantage you can seize upon once you're on your own. For example, during your "paid training," you may uncover an underserved market niche you can exploit when you're ready to make your move. Perhaps you will find a key competitor has a weak supply chain, broken manufacturing processes, poor product quality, or just plain lousy customer service. Oftentimes, having this information is all you need to gain an edge on the competition.

Once on your own, it will be more difficult (and certainly more expensive) to purchase a subscription to industry research that provides a comparable level of industry insider information that you are privy to while working for someone else. In addition, learning from the mistakes of others is equally as important as learning what companies do well. It's certainly much cheaper.

During your research, one of the things you should understand is the difference between a publicly traded and privately held company. There are pros and cons to both. Public companies issue stocks that are publicly traded and tend to be susceptible to the highs and lows of their quarterly earnings report and the stock market. Board members and top executives of publicly held companies focus on the preservation, growth, and how to maximize shareholder wealth.

Contrary to what you might think, actual earnings don't affect stock prices as much as financial analysts' *expectations* of performance. Share prices have already factored in economic forecasts, politics, global competition, and future earnings potential many months ago. As a result, you will find public companies can experience what I refer to as the *quarterly rollercoaster ride*.

WORKING FOR BIG COMPANIES

Do you want to work for a large, Fortune 500 company or a small company? Large corporations tend to pay better than smaller ones. They can afford it. Many successful, well-established, multinational corporations (MNCs) have accumulated hordes of cash to sustain them through business peaks and valleys so they can survive economic downturns. Larger companies recruit top-tier talent from the best schools to ensure ongoing success against their competition. Likewise, employee benefits are usually more generous when compared to what smaller organizations can afford due to their buying power. As an added incentive to attract the best and brightest, many offer profit-sharing programs, incentives, or bonuses based on individual and overall financial performance.

Check out your target company's stock price performance over the last year or two as part of your research—i.e., follow the money.

Publicly held companies whose stock prices fluctuate more than the norm tend to spend energy trying to maximize quarterly returns for their investors, as well as placate Wall Street analysts. This may lead to senior executive decisions that emphasize short-term gains but could hurt the company in the long term.

How does this affect you as an employee? If their financial performance was lower than what analysts "forecasted," the company's stock price could go down—significantly. When stock prices go down, so does its market value, which could lead to reactive measures by leadership to compensate. This is what you are seeing when you read a press release about a Fortune 500 company selling off one of its subsidiaries, announcing an across the board 10 percent layoff, or closing operations of an underperforming asset.

Mergers and acquisitions are other types of events that trigger mass layoffs. When companies combine, the newly formed organization is quick to recognize they don't need overlapping back-office functions. Part of the advantage of merging is the ability to reduce (or eliminate) duplicate shared services functions, such as Accounting, Human Resources, Supply Chain, Public Relations, IT . . . or duplicate manufacturing plants.

When a public company is purchased by a group of investors and takes the company private, this creates quite a different dynamic. A good example of this is when Dell acquired EMC. In this situation, the newly formed organization becomes insulated from the quarterly Wall Street rollercoaster. Since the new company is now privately held, executive leadership has the freedom to make better decisions based on more strategic, longer-term outcomes.

When public companies go private, it is usually by a *venture capital* or *private equity* firm. Venture capital firms typically invest in start-ups they believe have high growth potential. Private equity firms buy companies to gain total control. Both strive to maximize the value and total return on their investment and usually include a plan to take the company public within a few years via an IPO (Initial Public Offering). In the Dell-EMC situation, Dell partnered with a private equity firm, which protects them from making rash decisions and allows them to adopt a long-term outlook to grow/transform the business. These companies can be great to work for but they are usually very competitive and fast paced environments.

WORKING FOR SMALLER COMPANIES

Startups and smaller companies, on the other hand, can be a great place to work—especially if you join one that turns out to be a fast-growing company. People who thrive in an unstructured environment, are self-starters, and are unafraid to work with limited information should consider joining a smaller company. They have a flatter organizational hierarchy—i.e., fewer management layers— which means fewer approval signatures and little or no red tape to design, build, and deliver new products or services. Smaller companies are more flexible than larger ones and are able to react faster to changing market conditions. High-technology start-ups are great examples of companies that are agile like this. In addition, opportunities for career advancement are better in a startup because new positions are created as the company grows.

In short, the older and the bigger the company, the more bureaucracy and administrative overhead will have been created over the years. If you are not crazy about red tape and long lead times to produce change . . . then a smaller, nimbler environment may be a better fit for you.

Creating Your Resume

The first fifteen years of my professional career were in the staffing industry. As a recruiter, my job was to source qualified candidates for my clients. Hence, I gained plenty of experience reviewing and rewriting resumes that I could "sell" to my clients. Early on, I successfully hired out hundreds of people in a wide range of jobs— from engineers, technicians, accountants, analysts, project managers, designers, programmers, system administrators . . . to research scientists who specialized in computational fluid dynamics. The key to my success was my understanding of the industry and an ability to "sell" my candidates to my clients. I knew my customers were getting resumes from multiple suppliers for their openings, so my candidates' credentials had to stand out. I was very successful doing this and eventually moved my way up to vice president for the staffing company I worked for.

If you are putting together a resume for the first time, this section will help you. For recent graduates, people who are re-entering the workforce after a period of time, or those making a career change . . . I recommend you stress specific coursework, education, or training that is related to the role and industry you are applying for. This is especially important for those of you who are *changing* their occupation or industry. Also, include your GPA (if it is 3.0 or better), any certifications, career interests, and academic achievements. If you have little to no work experience, emphasize what work experience or internships you do have and any relevant projects or extracurricular activities.

If you are a more experienced job hunter, you will want to emphasize your skills, competencies, and relevant experience in the top section of your resume. Make it easy for recruiters to figure out what you do. For positions that require at least some experience— i.e., entry-level need not apply—hiring managers will weigh your skills and experience more heavily.

RESUME FORMAT

In the table below, I provide some structure on how to format your resume. For entry-level positions or for those without a lot of experience, let the recruiter/hiring manager know what your career objective is without having to guess. In the top section of your resume, list your best, most relevant qualifications, starting with the schools you attended in reverse chronological order—i.e., the most recent school first, the previous school if more than one—and when you completed your graduation requirements. If your graduation date is more than a couple of years ago, I don't recommend that you put the month or year. If you are applying for a sales and marketing position with an international company but have no work experience, include relevant classes like International Business, Marketing Promotion, Retail Merchandising, and Professional Sales & Sales Management.

Hiring managers are interested in how involved you were outside the classroom too. This helps them understand how well-rounded you are and gives them a glimpse of who you are and what matters to you. If you were co-captain of the color guard as part of your college marching band, it indicates you have some leadership skills. Likewise, if you won equestrian competitions, were high-school state champion in tennis, or little league world series runner-up . . . include it. Employers will recognize you are competitive and a winner. Many organizations today also place a lot of value on citizenship and involvement in community activities or charities.

Including information that tells the reader who you are enables them to connect with you. You would be surprised by how many recruiters and hiring managers were part of their high-school or college marching band and will automatically like you because they saw that in your resume.

ENTRY-LEVEL	EXPERIENCED
Career Objective	Professional Summary Statement
Education, GPA (if ≥ 3.0) + Coursework	Relevant skills to the position applied for
Experience (work and/or military)	Experience
Memberships, Associations*	Education
Extracurricular Activities, Sports*	Certifications, Professional Associations
Community Involvement*	Military Background*

* Optional Sections

Figure 7: Resume Formats

RESUME TIPS

The word "resume" is a French term that means to summarize or to sum up. This is good advice, especially in today's job market where there are scores of electronic job boards with hundreds of job postings and even more recruiters competing to fill them. This means you will need to put together a concise, cleanly formatted resume tailored to the target position.

Most recruiters spend very little time reviewing your resume unless they find something to compel them to read more. A survey conducted by job search site *TheLadders.com* claims recruiters spend only an average of about 6 seconds reviewing a résumé. (I must have been a little slow; I used to spend 10-15 seconds per resume.) This means you need to create a resume that gets your message across in 6 seconds or less. Furthermore, in those precious seconds, about 80 percent is focused on: Name, Education, Current Title & Company, current company Start & End Dates, previous Title & Company, and previous company Start & End Dates. Recruiters typically spent the remaining 20 percent of their résumé-scanning time looking for **keywords** that match the position description. Outside of keywords, according to the study, recruiters based their recommendations primarily on those six pieces of data.

To keep things in perspective, understand that the recruiter's job is to come up with the top two or three candidates to submit to the hiring manager. You could very well be competing with scores (if not hundreds) of other applicants for that one job opening. In addition, you can't rely on every recruiter to be intimately familiar with each job they are sourcing candidates for, so try to match the keywords and use similar language in your resume that was used in the job posting. Make it as easy as possible for the recruiter to identify you as a MATCH.

Also, if you have special skills, like you can read and write in three languages—English, French, and German—make sure those little pearls are in a highly visible spot in your resume.

RESUME DON'TS

Grammar: Be sure your grammar is correct and you have no structural errors in your resume. Hiring managers and recruiters have an uncanny knack for finding them. Don't give them an excuse to disqualify you for something controllable like that. Use your spellchecker, Grammerly.com (it's free), or have a trusted friend look over your resume. If you introduce an acronym in your resume, such as TLA (Three Letter Acronym), always include what it means (in parentheses) when introducing it for the first time. Also, don't overwrite things in your resume to sound smarter—i.e., saying *expeditious* instead of *swift*.

Adjectives: Never include adjectives when describing your position experience or accomplishments. Adjectives are subjective and often turns a recruiter or hiring manager off. Avoid phrases such as "significantly improved productivity" or "dramatically increased sales." Performance can be measured. When a hiring manager reads that, their knee-jerk reaction is to think, "I'll be the judge of what 'significantly' or 'dramatically' means." It's better to be specific when describing your achievements. Use language like "improved productivity by 28.2 percent" or "increased product sales by 112.4 percent over last year." This is fact-based, objective, and informative. Flowery language is fluff and frowned upon.

Exaggerate: Don't take credit for someone else's achievements, blatantly make things up, or exaggerate your accomplishments. Also, don't elevate your job title, embellish your level of responsibility, or overstate your experience. Claims such as "Led Project X to Accomplish Y" will be challenged. Good interviewers will ask you to specifically describe what your role was in Project X and who you reported to, what were your deliverables, and who reported to you. If you don't misrepresent yourself, then you will never have to cover your tracks or be exposed. The interview will be over quickly if you misrepresent your qualifications.

Short-term jobs: If you have only been with a company for a few months, be prepared to explain the short duration. Employers don't particularly like job-hoppers. They invest a lot of time, energy, and money training new hires and are not interested in wasting that investment. If you have worked for the same consulting firm or contracting agency for several assignments, then put the name of the consulting firm or agency, and in the same section, list the clients you were assigned to and the start/end dates of those assignments. It is accurate and acceptable to show you have been with the same consulting or contracting firm for multiple years and assigned to two or three different engagements. On a positive note, it shows you may have more well-rounded experience than someone who has only worked in the same position for the same period of time. Plus, it shows you adapt quickly to new situations.

Action Verbs: I recommend you list accomplishments and/or achievements under each Title & Company you have on your resume. This is much better than regurgitating the job description, which will bore the reader. Use an Action Verb –> Noun structure. Be aware of reusing the same action words throughout your resume. Take advantage of a thesaurus and mix your action verbs up, especially for action verbs such as transform, develop, create, author, initiate, improve, increase, reduce, deliver, or establish. Search online for "power words" that you can leverage to describe your accomplishments.

Hobbies: Unless your hobby is directly related to your career, it is best to leave it off. That said, it's probably okay to include the minor fact you won a gold medal in the 4×100-meter freestyle relay in the last Olympics or that you are a scratch golfer. Use your judgment.

References: Including a References section then adding "Provided upon request" under it is redundant. Don't bother. If they ask for references or professional recommendations, have them ready so you can provide them separately.

RESUME DOS

Career Objective: If you are attending a job fair, you may want to remove this section altogether or be more generic, such as "Entry-Level Mechanical Engineer." On the other hand, if you have as your objective "Seeking an Entry-Level Position as an Aerospace Engineer" and find a booth advertising for an Entry-Level Automotive Engineer, your objective will hurt you, not help you. In the case where you are submitting your resume online for a specific job posting, your objective should match the position title advertised. If your objective doesn't match the posting, you're giving the recruiter an excuse to think this position isn't your first choice and will move on to the next candidate who isn't settling. If your objective matches, the recruiter will check the box that you meet the requirement and will continue scanning the rest of your resume. When preparing your resume, never give recruiters an excuse to disqualify you.

Education: If you're a recent graduate, include the graduation month and year. If it has been more than six months from your graduation date, you might want to just put the year. Opinions differ regarding Grade Point Average (GPA) and whether to include it or not. Typically, I recommend including your GPA if it is greater than or equal to 3.0—especially for technical undergrads. (As a recruiter, I preferred candidate GPAs to be between 3.0 and 3.6 because I found they were able to communicate better with other carbon-based life forms.) The longer you are out of school, however, your GPA becomes less of a deciding factor. If you have more than five years of professional experience, you have already proven you can do the job, so you can leave it off your resume entirely.

Extracurricular Activities: Include any extracurricular activities that can help your cause. For example, include the little tidbit that you were chief design engineer on your college's *American Solar Challenge* entry that finished in the top five nationally this year. In addition, participation in a community service project in your local town would lead an employer to believe you are a solid citizen. By the same token, volunteering at a local hospital looks good if you are applying for a position in healthcare. People are people, so having been on a varsity sports team can also open doors for you, especially if the recruiter or hiring manager is a sports fan or a student-athlete too.

Experience: If you don't have a lot of experience, include what experience you do have. Underscore any transferrable skillsets. If the position calls for someone with analytical skills, then you should accentuate what relevant experience you have that required analytical skills. As much as possible, mirror the job description in your resume without being obvious about it. Use the same/similar language and keywords. Recruiters typically are pressured to produce results and want to find the miracle match as fast as possible so they can move on to the next opening. Make it easy for them to match the keywords and critical skillsets required for the position.

Job Hunting

There are many online job boards claiming they have the best site to help you find a job. The reality is between 40 to 80 percent of jobs today are still found through good old-fashioned networking. This means your chances of finding your next job by applying online does not have the highest probability payoff. For a typical entry-level position, your resume may be one of hundreds. Other surveys support this and claim less than 15 percent of positions are filled through job boards. In short, most jobs are filled either internally (and were never advertised) or through word of mouth.

Network with your friends, family, teachers, professors, and anyone else you believe can get the word out. If you find a job posting you are interested in, find out if there is someone in your circle of friends and family who works there too. Perhaps you will find someone who can put you in touch with the hiring manager.

I have listened to many conversations where one person mentioned XYZ Company is looking for a good widgeteer and someone else replied their neighbor, college buddy, or cousin happens to be a senior widgeteer who works there ... and the exchange of contact information began. As part of your search strategy, you can leverage online career networking sites such as LinkedIn and others like it. You can mine these sites to help you to find the kinds of positions you are most interested in and connect with people at the company of your choice. If you don't put the word out, no one can help you. Don't rely on chance or online job boards alone. Networking with people is still your best bet.

Assuming you have a great resume now, our next step is to help you perform well in the job interviewing process.

6 – Interviewing Skills

"Before anything else,
preparation is the key to success."
– Alexander Graham Bell

Congratulations! You got a call from a recruiter to schedule an interview. Good for you. Be sure to ask their name, how to spell it correctly, and listen carefully to their instructions. If you don't have something to write with handy, it's okay to ask the caller if they'll hold a few seconds while you grab pen and paper. Write everything down. You don't want to get any details wrong. Make sure you have the name and job title of the person who will be interviewing you next. If the recruiter didn't explain how the interviewing process will go, ask them. Thank the recruiter and let them know you look forward to speaking with him or her soon.

If you don't know much about the company that called, you should begin researching anything you can find on company history, recent news, anyone recently hired, executives who left the company, and relevant industry information. (See previous chapter for more tips.) Ask friends and family if they know anyone who has or currently works there to find out what the company is like. The more information you can get, the better prepared you will be.

During your research, if you find out the hiring manager used to work at Chrysler, it could help you connect if you mention your father retired as a manufacturing engineer at the Dodge Truck Plant.

Look for ways to connect. People normally want to hire other people like themselves. If there is any legit way you can slip inside their circle of trust, leverage it. (A word of caution—don't force this into the conversation if the discussion is moving in another direction. Only mention it if the opportunity arises.) You will be amazed to see how an interviewer's demeanor changes when you mention your connection to them or the company.

TELEPHONE / VIDEO INTERVIEW TIPS

If you are scheduling a telephone pre-screen interview first, you can relax a little because you have time to prepare. During the initial call from the recruiter, find out who will be doing the pre-screen interview. Even if it is the same recruiter who will be calling back, ask who the hiring manager is and what his or her job title is. This is good information that can help you with your research. Find out if anyone else will be on the call too.

If your telephone interview is with the hiring manager, all the better. Usually, the first call is someone from human resources or one of the hiring manager's direct reports. In the initial interview or pre-screen call, their general objective is to assess whether you might be a good "cultural fit" with the company and if you have decent communication skills or not so they can narrow down the list of candidates. To help you prepare for a telephone interview, I have provided you with some basic tips below.

1. A telephone pre-screen is still an interview. Treat it seriously. If you don't do well at this stage, you're done. There will be no second chance.
2. If it's an early appointment, wake up early, shower, get dressed, eat breakfast, have some coffee (or tea), and be ready to go.
3. If this is a video interview, dress as if you were going on a face-to-face interview.
4. Find somewhere to talk that is quiet and void of distractions.

5. Have your resume and cover letter in front of you in case they ask about your qualifications, education, or past job history.
6. Have your research notes in front of you because they usually ask what you know about the company.
7. Answer confidently and in a strong voice. Do not be overly soft-spoken or timid. This is your time to shine.

Do not chew gum, eat, or drink during the interview. It's okay to have a bottle of water handy, though. If you must drink, ask the interviewer if it is okay if you have a drink of water—sometimes if you're nervous in an interview, your throat will be dry. Otherwise, eating or drinking is a distraction and poor manners.

Keep a list of questions you anticipate the interviewer may ask along with your notes on how best to answer them. Be especially prepared for:

1. Why did you apply for this job?
2. What makes you qualified for this position?
3. Are you willing to travel?
4. Can you relocate?
5. When can you be available to start?

Always have a list of questions to ask at the end of the interview. If you don't have any questions, it is a red flag for recruiters you are not prepared or don't care enough to know more about the position or the company.

Walk about when you're on the phone. It helps dispense nervous energy and helps keep you focused. I have a habit of pacing myself. Just make sure you're not wandering around in an area where you can trip over something!

If they ask what your salary requirements are, divert the question to ask what the salary range is for the position. If they press, say you are negotiable and trust the company will pay fair market wages. It's more important at this stage to determine whether the position is a good fit for you. Money will come later. I provide more on salary negotiations later.

PREPARING FOR A FACE-TO-FACE INTERVIEW

Now that you made it past the telephone pre-screen, you need to prepare for the face-to-face interview. First, however, we need to cover some things that can kill you in a job interview. Assume you are competing against other well-qualified candidates who are also smart, willing to work hard, and be punctual. As a hiring manager, if an applicant I am interviewing committed any of the faux pas shown below, I would begin looking for other reasons to disqualify them. Below is a short list of all too common **interviewing mistakes**:

1. Poor appearance
2. Arriving late
3. Being unprepared
4. Inability to articulate your responses
5. Misrepresenting your experience, skills, or education

DRESS FOR SUCCESS

As a part of your research on the company and its culture, find out what the dress code is. It's normal to ask the recruiter what people wear to work there. Remember, you're not going nightclubbing, you are interviewing for a job that will be your livelihood. Use good judgment when it comes to selecting your fashion choices.

If you are interviewing for an office job, it is best to err on the safe side. I recommend a conservative business suit for both men and women (unless you are interviewing to be a fashion designer or lead vocalist in a band, in which case it's better to be your creative self). Otherwise, don't give anyone an excuse to *not like* what you're wearing. As a rule of thumb, if it's a very casual workplace, dress one level up from what the minimum attire is, and you should be fine.

Make sure to give yourself extra time to arrive at your interview just in case Murphy's Law of Commuting kicks in—i.e., "If anything can go wrong, it will." Life will throw you little twists, such as a car accident will occur before your very eyes while on your way to the interview or the road you need to take is closed for construction or there is a presidential motorcade in your path at precisely the time you are supposed to arrive for your interview. To be safe, it's a good idea to arrive thirty minutes early. It doesn't hurt to sit in your car for fifteen minutes or so while you use the time to rehearse your answers to anticipated questions one more time. You should also be more relaxed because you're not being rushed.

If your interview is downtown, ask where to park, how much it costs, and if there is any parking validation (i.e., they stamp your parking ticket so you can park for free). Allow some extra time to find a parking spot. (See Murphy.) Find out what side of the building the lobby is located on if you are supposed to meet the recruiter there. Many office buildings have a front security desk and require you to provide identification (such as driver's license) to get a temporary access badge. Lastly, if you sense it is appropriate, ask for the recruiter's direct telephone number and/or the main lobby number—just in case you run into a detour or get disoriented because you have never been to that part of town before.

THE FACE-TO-FACE INTERVIEW

The next time you go to your local restaurant, library, or shopping mall . . . sit and do a bit of people watching for a while. Take note what people are wearing. If you see someone wearing a printed t-shirt, rest assured they are advertising to the world what they want you to think about them. For example, a guy wearing a t-shirt saying "Come and Take It" with a picture of a plastic straw is probably not an environmentalist. Some folks may tell you wearing a printed t-shirt is all about expressing their individualism or to showcase their style. What they are really doing is making a statement about who they are, the things they like, or what they believe in.

As you watch people walk by, ask yourself if they are dressed professionally or casually? Observe how people walk. Are they strolling along without a care in the world? Is their head down and not making eye contact? Or are they striding confidently ahead like they are on a mission? How do they sit? Is their posture straight and tall or are they slouching? Watch people involved in a conversation. Are they animated as they talk? Is one person listening attentively and the other person preoccupied and only half listening? Or are they both engaged and laughing? What do you want others' impression of you to be?

How you look, how you walk, how you sit, how you talk, and your body language all are components of your *brand*. Think of your persona as *Me, Incorporated*. Behave as if you were in business for yourself. When *you* walk into an employer's lobby, you are an unknown. Therefore, your appearance, how you carry yourself, how you sit, where you sit, how you stand, the way you walk, the expression on your face, how you are dressed, how you fix your hair . . . everything you do is a representation of your *brand*.

First impressions are lasting impressions. In the article *The 7 Things Interviewers Notice First* by Jada A. Graves, she says arrival time, attire, body language, communication style, preparedness, enthusiasm, and qualifications are the top things interviewers look at to evaluate talent. Be aware of your brand as you enter the room with your interviewers.

As the interview begins, the recruiter will likely start out the conversation telling you a little about the company. Even though you may be excited to share what research you've done, NEVER INTERRUPT the interviewer or try to dominate the conversation! Interrupting or talking over someone else who is speaking is rude. If you interrupt someone, you are essentially conveying you don't care what he or she is talking about and what you have to say is more important than what they're saying.

When an interviewer asks a tough question, a helpful trick is to repeat the question back to the recruiter. This can buy you a little time to give yourself a chance to think before you answer a difficult or unanticipated question. It also gives you an opportunity to make sure you understood the question correctly and provides you some precious time to focus on answering the question thoughtfully. This is much better than blurting out something off the top of your head, which can make you sound like you are rambling on if you are not careful.

Some interviewers love the sound of their own voice. My advice is to let the interviewer talk if he or she gets on a roll. As I mentioned earlier, interrupting someone is bad form and especially so if you want to make a good first impression. In my experience, some of the best interviews were the ones where I hardly said a word. The interviewer talked throughout the entire process about this and that, oftentimes straying off topic. If you find yourself in a situation where the interviewer loves to hear themselves talk . . . let them. They will love you.

You should also have a short list of questions prepared. Don't be discouraged if you are speaking with a recruiter and not the hiring manager. If the recruiter does not have deep knowledge about the job priorities and day-to-day responsibilities, you can still ask questions like how the position became available and if this is a new position or a backfill—i.e., replacing someone who was promoted, transferred, or quit. If it is a new position, ask why it was created. If it is a backfill, ask what they want the next person who fills this role to do differently? Ask about the culture and what a typical day would be like if you were hired.

I also believe it is acceptable to ask for immediate feedback. If you are interested in the position and want the job . . . tell them so. You can politely ask the interviewer if he or she believes you have what it takes to move on in the process. If everything seems favorable, ask what the next steps are. If the interviewer's answer isn't a <u>Yes</u>, then anything else they say afterward probably means it's a <u>No</u>. If you receive anything less than positive feedback, you have nothing to lose by asking what areas of your qualifications were of concern so you can improve your performance next time.

If you make it past the initial interview and are scheduled for a second interview . . . Congratulations! When the recruiter calls to set up a second or final interview, have your notepad ready to write down the details as we discussed earlier.

Now we need to talk about what specific interview questions to expect and how to interview well.

Interview Questions

In the previous section, we discussed the types of questions a recruiter or hiring manager may ask you during an interview. In this section, I provide some background and advice on how to answer these questions:

1. Tell us a little about yourself.
2. Why do you want to work here?
3. What are your strengths?
4. What are your weaknesses?
5. Describe your ideal work environment.
6. Do you prefer to work in teams or as an individual contributor?
7. What are your career goals?
8. Where do you see yourself in one/two/three/five years from now?
9. What is the best job (or supervisor) you have had so far and why?

BEGINNING THE INTERVIEW

As the interview begins, I suggest you try to build some rapport with the recruiter, hiring manager, or panel. You will have to trust your Spidey senses here. A little courtesy conversation makes for a pleasant rest of the interview. (They need to know you are a person and not a robot.) You can ask safe questions like how long he or she has worked for the company and why they think it's a great place to work. Another easy question is to ask where the interview is originally from and how long they've lived in your town.

When you sense the conversation is transitioning to the interview portion, an important question to ask that sets you up well is "I have read the job description, but they don't always include what is most important to the hiring manager . . . What qualifications would the ideal candidate have for this position?" Knowing the ideal qualifications they are looking for at the beginning of the interview helps you tailor your responses throughout the rest of the interview. By association, the interviewer may even subliminally associate the ideal candidate with you because, if they are looking for a self-starter, you will shape your answers to emphasize how you take initiative or are willing to do over and above what is required to complete the mission.

Don't forget—you are interviewing them too. You are interviewing the company to see if it's a fit with your personality, career goals, values, or interests. You are interviewing your potential future boss to assess whether your personalities will mesh or clash. If you don't think you'll like your boss, it'll probably be tough to be successful there. (Of course, if you are hungry and need to pay the rent, you may be willing to put up with less than a perfect fit—for now.)

Be prepared for the typical interview questions. Practice and preparedness breed confidence. Again, you can buy yourself a little more time by repeating the questions back to the interviewer to make sure you understood the question correctly. Don't misrepresent your background or experience. If you try to make up things on the fly, they will know. Likewise, if you are insecure, interviewers will easily spot that too. If you are nervous in the interview and your voice is shaking, you have nothing to lose to by saying, "Pardon me if I sound a bit nervous . . . This job means a lot to me." They may be more patient with you because you showed a little vulnerability. However, if you are prepared and your answers are well articulated and crisp, they will notice that as well. That's ideally what they are looking for.

In the sections that follow, I provide suggestions on how to answer the typical interview questions hiring managers ask. Also included are sample responses for you to consider. Of course, you will have to make the answers match your personal style and situation. Use your best judgment and adapt to the situation you find yourself in.

TELL US A LITTLE ABOUT YOURSELF.

This is usually the first question in the interview and is your make or break moment. No pressure, eh? First impressions are huge in an interview. Research shows the first fifteen seconds determine whether you get the job or not . . . and the rest of the interview is just Kabuki Theater. On the other hand, I have interviewed more than a few people who stumbled at the beginning of an interview who later recovered well and ended up getting a job offer. So I'm not saying a minor slip at the beginning of an interview is unrecoverable. What I am saying is it is highly advisable to be well prepared so you can give yourself every advantage—especially if there are several strong candidates the hiring manager has to choose from.

Your response to this question should be a well-rehearsed **Elevator Speech** that you can recite on demand. This is your big chance to make your pitch about you . . . and your story should be adapted to segue deftly into making the case as to why you are a great candidate for this position. This is <u>not</u> the time to tell your life story. Stick to the script. Keep your response professional. Remember, this is a job interview, so the interviewer is really asking, "What should I know about you that will help me decide between you and the other candidates?"

After this question, I suggest you try to ask, "I read the job description for this position . . . but sometimes the hiring manager may be looking for certain talents that may not have been captured in the posting. Are there qualifications you are looking for that may not be in the job description?" Sometimes this question can be the difference-maker. If you are able to maneuver the interview to a point where you can ask this question, it can't hurt to know what the hiring manager really wants, right?

WHY DO YOU WANT TO WORK HERE?

Usually, the next question hiring managers like to ask are "Why do you want to work for our company?" or "Why are you interested in this position?" to determine if you are just looking for a paycheck or actually interested in the role. For mid- to senior-level positions, interviewers may ask why you want to work for them to see if you have done your research and to determine what your motivation is for applying. However, you still need to be prepared with a solid answer even for entry-level positions. Your responses could be similar to the ones below:

"When I saw your ad for this position, I thought it was a great fit with my career goals. One of my best friends works as a Technical Support Analyst, and she told me all about her job. She said it's a great way to learn about the organization and learn more about the

IT systems used there. I am very interested in working in technical support because of the learning opportunities it provides. Besides, I have heard good things about your company, and for me, I want to feel good about the company I work for. I have always been interested in technology, and your company is one of the fastest growing tech firms in town. I'd like to be a part of that."

"After I first learned about this position, I started asking around. Eventually, I was able to speak with someone who used to work for your company, and he only had good things to say. I put a lot of myself into what I do, and it was good to hear this company believes in investing in people who want to grow. He also said your business is growing fast, so that could mean I may have the opportunity to move up once I have proven myself."

WHAT ARE YOUR STRENGTHS?

This is a bit of a trick question. You should answer this question confidently without appearing brash or overconfident. Typical strengths include things like you are a team player, quick learner, trustworthy, flexible, high integrity, organized/planner, good communicator, reliable, likable, problem solver (versus someone who brings their problems to their boss to figure out), creative, and passionate about (fill in the blank).

Be prepared to list your top two or three strengths and be ready to provide examples of why they are strengths. Describe situations at work or school where you demonstrated these strengths. For the most part, I discourage stating your biggest strength is you are a <u>hard worker</u> because that should be a given. Everyone interviewing for this job should be a hard worker. However, if you want to say you are a hard worker, qualify that with something like, "While I am a hard worker, I also believe in working smart. I analyze the task I am assigned, plan the work, collaborate with those who may be impacted, and execute the task to the best of my ability."

Another key strength is being a good <u>communicator</u>—both oral and written. If you can't communicate well, your career will be limited. I have worked with people who were brilliant people but worked in a bubble. No one in management knew about them because they were not good at socializing with their peers or knew how to manage up. Being a poor communicator can hold you back. For example, if you don't coordinate your tasks with others who are working on the same project as you or collaborate with other departments who may be impacted by what you are doing, your project is at a risk of failure. You need to think about how the tasks you are working on affects others. Tell the interviewer, if you were working on a team project, that you would seek input from others to get their perspective to help you all be successful.

WHAT ARE YOUR WEAKNESSES?

I am not particularly fond of this question, but it will be asked. Interviewers may disguise this question by asking: "What area would you most like to change about yourself/strengthen?" or "Tell me about your blind spots?" or "Tell me about a mistake you made, how you corrected the situation, and what you learned from it." or "What would you say you need to work on?"

How you respond to this question is very important. While I realize nobody wants to present a negative image of themselves, to say you have no weakness is disingenuous. And don't answer this question with "I am a perfectionist . . ." or "I work too hard . . ." because the hiring manager will know you are trying to snow them. The interviewer wants to know something about you that you are not good at (yet). He or she wants to know if you are self-aware and can be honest about assessing your strengths and weakness.

When conducting your personal inventory, think about something you have struggled with in the past. Your "weakness" could be speaking in front of large groups of people or waiting until the last moment to meet a deadline. Explain what steps you have taken to overcome this or how you are still working on it to get better.

Another way to handle this question is to think of every weakness as the downside of a corresponding strength. If you are someone who takes great pride in your quality of work and/or likes to get a lot done, then you might have trouble delegating tasks. To overcome this, you can explain you have learned one person can accomplish only so much, while a team can accomplish much more. You can explain that you always look for the smartest way to complete a task and delegate work to others if they can do it at least 75 percent as well as you. Using this as a rule of thumb, you may only have to re-work 25 percent of a task instead of having to take on the whole effort yourself. Besides, over time, you will have empowered others to do the task without help.

DESCRIBE YOUR IDEAL WORK ENVIRONMENT.

This question is asked because the hiring manager is listening for cues to determine whether you work best on your own or if you are motivated by interacting as part of a team. In short, the interviewer wants to know what motivates you. If you provide an example where you worked for months locked in a bunker designing vision systems for robot-assisted surgery, the interviewer will most likely classify you as an introvert and surmise you work best as an individual contributor.

Conversely, if you tell the interviewer, "I loved my internship with Avance Marketing because I was allowed to work directly with customer focus groups to solicit their opinions on an upcoming product release," this would lead the interviewer to think you are a people person and get your energy from interacting with others.

WHAT ARE YOUR CAREER GOALS?

Remember who your audience is when answering this question. The hiring manager wants to know how your goals match with his or her immediate needs. Start out by answering what your immediate goals are in some detail and then move on to describe your long-term goals. It may sound obvious, but your short-term goals should be centered on the position for which you are interviewing.

If the situation allows, you can talk about your ultimate career goals too. In that case, you may want to explain why you are interested in your particular career path and explain what steps you are prepared to take to achieve your goals. For example, if you say you want to be in management someday, you can frame that like the response below.

> *In the beginning, I will be focusing on mastering my profession—learning as much as possible about my role, what my job means in the bigger scheme of things, and earning my certification. Over time, I would like to develop some management skills by leading some projects. Also, I am constantly in learning mode. I am an avid reader, would like to attend leadership conferences if I can, and eventually earn an MBA.*

Describing your plan to achieve your goals demonstrates an ability to think analytically and that you are taking your career seriously. If hired, your manager will know he or she will have to keep you challenged and find ways for you to develop and grow with the company.

WHY DID YOU LEAVE YOUR LAST JOB?

If you have already been in the workforce, your interviewer will likely ask, "Why are you looking to make a change?" This is a critical question. Never, ever, say anything negative about a previous boss or employers. Don't get personal in your response either. The term "six degrees of separation" is the theory that says we are all connected to any other person through no more than five additional acquaintances. The world is much smaller than you think. You don't know who knows whom or who is related to whom. Besides, you have nothing to gain by being negative and will instead be seen as a potential problem child.

If you are still working or left your last job voluntarily, you can answer this question in several ways that can put you in a positive light.

> *I do enjoy my current job, in the sense my boss and co-workers are great and very supportive, but I believe I can do more and am ready for my next challenge.*

I recently earned my technical certification and want to leverage that, my degree, and experience to get to the next level in my field. I am unable to do that where I am now.

I am interested in a new challenge and want to use my skills and experience in a different capacity than in the past.

I really was not considering a change, but a friend recommended this job to me. After a bit of research on your company and the industry, I find myself intrigued by its growth potential. This sounds like an exciting opportunity and a great fit with my qualifications.

Even though I survived the first two rounds of layoffs, eventually I was laid-off from my last position when my job was eliminated due to a recent merger.

WHO IS THE BEST JOB YOU HAVE HAD AND WHY?

This is one of the better questions to be asked. Focus on the positives—not the negatives. Describe the type of job or role where you can thrive. Let the interviewer know how your previous boss brought out the best in you and drove you to accomplish more than you initially thought possible. When answering this question, consider responses such as:

I have been fortunate to have worked for some excellent managers. They taught me to "manage up" to ensure I was aligned with their expectations. We met regularly to communicate status on projects to which I was assigned.

I enjoy working in teams and am willing to take on additional responsibility. My last boss supported this and would regularly rotate responsibilities to lead new projects.

I always strive to communicate with my boss and appreciate when they acknowledge my hard work and dedication. Then again, I also appreciate honest, constructive feedback so I can improve my performance.

My favorite boss was a very busy person and demanded high-quality work products from her direct reports. She did not have time to micro-manage her team because of how much responsibility she had, so I learned to listen carefully and write down her directives and work to complete the task with minimal supervision.

WHAT TYPE OF SALARY ARE YOU LOOKING FOR?

This is a tricky question. I strongly recommend you research what the market is paying for the type of job you are applying for so you know what salary expectation you should have. As an entry-level applicant, you will have less leverage than a more experienced candidate—unless you are in a field that is in high demand. Or if you were the project lead for your college's top ten finish in NASA's Human Exploration Rover Challenge, you can command a higher salary. Otherwise, temper your expectations to slightly higher than the average.

Note that whatever your salary is when you start a new job, this will be the baseline that all your future raises or promotions will be calculated against. In your salary negotiations, if you blurt out a salary expectation that's too high, you could immediately eliminate yourself from consideration. If your salary request is too low, they may wonder what is wrong with you and move on to the next applicant . . . or worse, they hire you, and soon, you find out all your peers make 25 percent more than you do.

If you will pardon the poker analogy, I recommend you don't show your cards first. Let the employer make the first gambit so you can find out what salary range you are working with. Once you know what their salary range is for the position, and what the market is for your chosen profession, you can counter this question with something like the examples shown below.

Given you are one of the market leaders in the industry, I am confident you will make a fair offer. What is the salary range you have established for this position?

Based on my research of similar positions in this area and industry, employers are paying between X and Y. Is this the salary range budgeted for this position?

All I can expect is a salary consistent with what your current employees are making at the same level. I believe I can be an asset to your department and would love to hear your offer.

What if the company offers $10k more than what you were going to ask for? If you had made the first move, you would have left money on the table. If the organization offers $10k less than your target, but you still really want the job, you can ask them how close they can come to your number. If they meet you halfway, you can ask if there are other compensation options, such as a car allowance, quarterly profit sharing, flexible work hours, additional paid time off (PTO), matching funds for retirement, or other benefits. In the end, it is up to you to determine if the compensation package meets your needs.

Note the average salary you can find on Salary.com is just a starting point in understanding what the market might bear for that job classification. Statistically, the majority of employees are making less or more than the average. Larger companies can afford to pay top college graduates significantly higher compensation than the average, thus skewing the average salary calculation. Conversely, smaller companies oftentimes cannot offer top salaries. Understanding that, don't be crushed if the market isn't exactly great at the time you are interviewing. There is also a bit of luck involved regarding the timing of your job hunt. For example, what if you're interviewing for a pharmaceutical sales job and a big recall was just announced for a drug the company makes? Through no fault of your own, market conditions can change at any time.

The reality is if you find yourself facing a less than ideal job market, don't be too proud to take a job that pays lower than what you believe the market can bear. Be patient. The economy giveth and it taketh away. On a positive note, you will gain experience, and you never know . . . in a year or two, you may get promoted and—because you did all the things you were supposed to be doing to excel at your job—you get a big, fat raise. Or you may find market conditions have changed in your favor, and you find your occupation in high demand. Be patient and stay focused on the path you want to be on. Persevere.

7 – COMMUNICATION SKILLS

"Intelligence, knowledge, or experience
are important and might get you a job,
but strong communication skills
are what will get you promoted."
– Mireille Guiliano

As a former recruiter, I wish I had a dollar for every time a hiring manager said communication skills were the most important qualification for their opening. Yes, there is a direct relationship between how far you succeed in your career and how well you communicate. If you don't continually work to expand your communication skills—both oral and written—then you are placing a limitation on your success. The good news is this is something you can control. You can always improve your communication skills. Becoming a great communicator is a skill that can be learned. For many of us, it takes hard work and a lot of practice. The sooner you start, the faster this can become one of your strengths and begin making a difference in your life.

It takes two to communicate. The communication process consists of a Sender and Receiver. If you are the Sender, be aware that what you say will be "interpreted" by the Receiver. A great example of how this works is a game you may have played in school called *The Telephone Game*. This is the game where the teacher whispers a short message to the first student in the first row of the classroom and tells the student to pass it on to the next person. By the time the message gets to the last student in the last row, the story has changed dramatically. In the world of work, people do the same thing. People can't help but add their own commentary, flair, and flavor to the story in order to spice it up for the next telling.

It's amazing how small changes in how someone interprets an announcement about a new policy can evolve over time to the point the intent of the original message is lost. Rumors gone wild can undermine the purpose of the original communication.

Assume whatever you say or write will be interpreted and decoded using the unique decoder ring of the Receiver, which may not necessarily match your original intent. The lesson to be learned is to carefully craft your communications that will be sent out to others. Understand who the Receivers are—your audience—and use clear language they will understand. If it is going out to a larger group, call your friend in corporate communications or someone you trust to sanity check your draft. Getting someone else's point of view can be very helpful in avoiding a miscommunication that could be embarrassing.

"The most important single ingredient in the formula of success is knowing how to get along with people."
– Theodore Roosevelt

HONING YOUR COMMUNICATION SKILLS

It is just as important to be able to communicate well with those above you and below your level in an organization. If you are ineffective as a communicator or act like a hermit, you will never be top-of-mind when leadership is succession planning.

Have you listened to yourself on a video or audio recorder? How do you sound when you speak? Do you think you are effective at communicating? Can you influence people to your way of thinking? Does your passion come through? Are people able to follow along with what you are trying to say? Do you sometimes find yourself at a loss for words?

Like anything you do, practice makes perfect. If you feel like your vocabulary isn't as extensive as you want it to be, then look up every word you don't know in a dictionary (or online) and practice using it in your conversations for the next week or two. If you want to improve your skills, watch and emulate people who you believe are great communicators.

Books that focus on customer service and insight selling can help you the most. Learning how to provide great customer service and sell your ideas at work are invaluable assets. Regardless of occupation—from tech nerd to advertising rep—we all can benefit by having better communication skills. No one is exempt. Everybody needs to have decent communication skills. Regardless of whether you are presenting a business case to initiate a new project, introduce a new product line, or selling services, it all boils down to how well you can convince others to see things your way . . . and convince them to take action. If you are in sales, your success stems from your ability to build long-term relationships with your customer, understand their business, and propose solutions that solve their business needs.

In order to understand what your customers want or need, you'll have great listening skills. We already discussed how to be a good Sender, so now let's focus on being a good Receiver. It is amazing how many people don't listen well.

LISTENING SKILLS

Habit 5 of Covey's *7 Habits of Highly Successful People* is "Seek first to understand, then be understood." If you take the time to observe others in conversation, you will learn that productive exchanges are when one person is talking at a time and the other person is actively listening, trying to understand what is being said. Conversely, there are those one-sided affairs where one person is talking and you can see the other person fidgeting and can barely wait to respond. Instead of actively listening, the Receiver is really a "Pending Sender" instead of listening.

You'll never learn anything if you're the one talking all the time. You already know what your opinion is, so become an active listener.

Show respect for others and pay attention when someone is speaking to you. Give them your undivided attention. Maintain eye contact and periodically acknowledge their message without interrupting. Make sure your body language shows you are engaged—i.e., don't look over your shoulder with one foot in the doorway. And for goodness sakes, don't pull out your phone.

Once the speaker has finished, keep an open mind and try to see things from their viewpoint. Show them you understand and think before you respond. Restrain yourself from starting your reply with a "Yeah, but . . ." and instead try saying "I understand your point; would you consider another way of trying to accomplish that?" If you disagree, focus the discussion on challenging the idea or approach, but don't attack them personally. Be objective and provide feedback that isn't judgmental. You can catch more flies with honey than with vinegar.

A great book on this topic is *Getting More: How to Negotiate to Achieve Your Goals in the Real World* by Stuart Diamond. In his book, Diamond suggests you try to understand the pictures in the head of the person with whom you are negotiating so you can see things from their point of view. Understanding what the person on the other side of the table wants can help you build a bridge to an agreement. Another great resource for acquiring similar skills is the timeless *How to Win Friends and Influence People* by Dale Carnegie. Even though this book was originally published in 1936, these principles apply just as readily today. If you drive a lot, it's available on audiobook as well.

Body Language

Communication consists of more than your rate of speech, your tone, and the words you use. There are three core elements that make up the **7-38-55 Rule**. This rule is based on research by Albert Mehrabian, Professor Emeritus of Psychology at UCLA, which says 7 percent of your communication is the spoken word, 38 percent is your tone of voice, and 55 percent is your body language. Hence, your body language is the most important form of communication. This includes the way you walk, the gestures you make, your posture, and your facial expressions while you talk. Everything non-verbal about you conveys subtle and sometimes subliminal signals to the Receiver. There are many good books on body language, but I will share a few common body language guidelines that could help you in your career.

If you sit with your arms crossed and/or legs crossed, people may perceive you are feeling defensive or you are holding something back. On the other hand, some people may just be in a cold room and cross their arms trying to stay warm, so keep in mind context—i.e., your situation and surroundings. Another indicator is how you sit. If you are talking to someone who has their legs and body faced away from you (or toward the door), it is a signal they would rather not be having the conversation. They might even be planning their getaway. Then again, if someone is leaning toward you, it is a nonverbal way of telling you he or she is interested in what you are saying.

When in a meeting with others at work, sit straight. Slouching tends to make people think you are lazy, uninterested, or don't care. Conversely, sitting far forward may come off as assertive or aggressive—unless you are mirroring the leader's body language—then it looks like you're engaged. Pointing or chopping motions when you talk also indicates aggression. Be aware of how you are being perceived.

When someone speaks to you, face the person talking and maintain respectful eye contact. Do your best to not appear distracted or restless because people will think you would rather be somewhere else. And don't pick up your phone and start texting in a meeting. I've been in meetings where someone was playing Candy Crush. It shows they are tone-deaf to good meeting etiquette. Not good.

Lastly, please smile. People who smile display confidence and have the appearance of genuineness and warmth. If you don't smile, you may be perceived as grim, unimaginative, distant, or unfriendly. Smiling is free. You can make a friend with just a smile.

COMMUNICATING ON THE JOB

The best method of communication is, has always been, and will always be face to face. People who meet face to face find it easier to establish working relationships with others, solve misunderstandings faster, and in general, experience better outcomes.

If you can't meet face to face with a group of co-workers, then a video or audio conference call is the next best thing. In conference calls, you can share your ideas or discuss the problem at hand with others and get real-time interaction, which solves problems much quicker. They will "hear" your tone and passion along with the words. If you're on a telephone call with a co-worker, at least you will be able to have the back and forth interaction where you can be creative or problem-solve.

The next best form of communication is live chat or instant messenger—i.e., collaboration platforms. While you do lose the "tone of voice" factor that conveys feeling, at least communication is still two-way. Text messaging is a step down from chat but still has that back-and-forth exchange real-time.

Lastly, email is a necessary and accepted form of business communication. However, email is the least preferred form of communication because it is a one-way message. Emails are also susceptible to misinterpretation, misunderstandings, and often used to cover one's bottom instead of advancing the ball forward. At work, people abuse and misuse email. Studies contend corporate employees spend as much as half their working day on email. That's a lot of time in lost productivity. To help you manage this necessary evil, below are a few friendly **email guidelines** to keep you from creating man-made drama.

- If you see more than three emails go back and forth among participants, go and talk face to face or set up a meeting to work things through. Try not to spam everybody.
- Do not reply to all to say "thank you" or copy people who don't have a need to know. If you want to thank someone, thank that person—not everyone on the distribution.

- If you are upset, wait before you send an email. I recommend a 24-hour cooling off period. If you still feel compelled to send your message after then, at least try to soften the tone so you don't sound like a raving lunatic.

You should be aware that emails and text messages are the property of the company you work for. You have no privacy when it comes to using any corporate collaboration systems. Don't send anything electronically—via text, chat, or email—that could embarrass you. A good rule of thumb is not to send anything you wouldn't want to show your boss or co-workers.

Succeeding in
Your Job

8 – TRAITS OF SUCCESSFUL PEOPLE

"I find that the harder I work,
the more luck I seem to have."
– Thomas Jefferson

As you study successful people's behaviors and habits, you will find there is a consistency in what they do. Consider these repeated behaviors a "system" that can be replicated. You may think it's only common sense, but there really is no such thing as *common sense*. If there was, it would be more commonplace, don't you think?

In the sections that follow, I will explain the common traits successful people tend to have, how they benefit you, and how to apply them to your situation. Try to design these traits into the way you think, act, and interact with others. These tips are based in part on an article I read in Forbes, *14 Things Every Successful Person Has in Common* by Dan Schawbel, as well as my own experience.

Behaviors of Successful People

Successful people carefully plan their lives and careers. If you don't have a master plan, your chances of achieving what you want out of life are limited because, well, you haven't even figured out what success looks like. With a well-thought-out career plan, you can execute your strategy in order to accomplish what you want out of life. Conversely, folks without a plan could end up stuck running in place their whole life. They will wake up, waste away the day, and never feel the sense of satisfaction you get when you accomplish your goals.

HAVE GOALS

Set goals that are SMART—i.e., Specific, Measurable, Achievable, Realistic, and Time-bound. An example of a SMART goal is "Become the top producing salesperson in your region before your twenty-fifth birthday." Now you need to figure out how you will accomplish this. Below is a sample list of tactics you could carry out to achieve this goal.

1. Become the <u>expert</u> in your field by finding a mentor at your company—preferably the most successful person—and learning everything you can.
2. <u>Network</u> with your counterparts at your closest competitors and share best practices, strengths, and weakness of the products or services you sell.
3. Work with your own marketing, product management, and engineering teams to <u>learn</u> every aspect about the product you sell.
4. Talk with and <u>get to know your customers</u>. Learn what their challenges are, what problems they are trying to solve, and what their strategic plan is for success.
5. Consistently <u>outsell everybody else</u> in your region— including your competitors.
6. Learn how to <u>teach</u> others, how to build high performing teams, and document processes to ensure repeatable success.

If you accomplish all these steps, then the chances are very good you will achieve your goal. Incidentally, make sure you are helping others along the way too. Also, one of the most valuable attributes successful people possess is they are usually likable. If you disrespect others and aren't friendly and helpful, you will find that kind of bad behavior will hold you back. No one wants to work with a jerk, so don't be that person.

MAKE YOUR OWN LUCK

Luck springs from hard work sustained over time and smartly positioning yourself for success. Unlike the movies, you won't miraculously get lucky and get rich quick. Success comes to those who plan well, are consistent, and are persistent. Successful people understand this. They have the discipline to do at least one thing every single day to put them in a better position to be *lucky*. Luck is not an accident. Fortunes are created where preparation meets opportunity.

Unlucky people miss out on opportunities because they are too consumed with something else. One example is if you obsess about being lonely. You may go to parties on a mission to find the perfect partner and end up missing out on opportunities to make new friends. On the other hand, if you go to the party with an open mind and a willingness to make new friends, you may meet people you genuinely like.

Expanding your circle of friends could increase your chances of making even more friends and meeting other people . . . and one day, perhaps even your future spouse! Besides, it's probably better to be friends first anyway, right? Lucky people are more relaxed and open and see what is there rather than what they are looking for.

DO MORE THAN WHAT IS EXPECTED

Some people believe they are owed something when they arrive on the job. They think all they need to do is show up to get good grades, be promoted, or make the big bucks. You cannot skip the steps, and nothing is free.

Successful people do the little extra—whether it is cleaning up their work area, organizing the tool room, or creating a business plan for the department. They accomplish this during work, on their own time, or after hours. If you have chosen the right profession—one that doesn't seem so much like work—then it won't seem so bad because it's what you like to do. If you produce quality work, this "extra credit" will be recognized by your boss, adds to your brand, and will benefit your career in the long run.

TAKE RESPONSIBILITY

Being accountable is taking responsibility for everything you do. Being responsible means accepting the obligation to complete the tasks assigned to you—no excuses. Responsible people are accountable and take ownership if things go wrong. If they mess up, they admit it. As part of your growth, it's important to know who you are and what your values are. With this foundation, you establish a reputation for integrity.

From now on, tell yourself, if I make a mistake, then I will take responsibility for it. This doesn't mean you have to simply fall on the sword and accept defeat. It means if you make a mistake, learn from it. If you miss completing an important step in a work task, create or update relevant procedures to reduce the risk of you or your successor making the same error in the future. Every time you misstep or have a near miss, be sure to evaluate whether you need to take corrective action so you won't repeat the error. It may sound funny, but making new and unusual mistakes aren't as bad as continually making the same ones.

BUILD RELATIONSHIPS

For the most part, successful people are not as territorial as you might think. They continually seek to build mutually beneficial relationships with others. Most successful people network well, and even if they are not friends, they know of each other by name or reputation within their respective industries. They associate themselves with others who have common interests and, like them, are striving to get ahead the right way. In this way, they can increase their sphere of influence and help their friends become successful too. They subscribe to the abundance mindset, which is what former president John F. Kennedy meant when he said "a rising tide lifts all boats."

In your career, you may discover some of your co-workers all came from the same former employer. You may find a core group of people move from one company to another together or have worked together at different times in their career. When a new leader joins a company, he or she usually doesn't know anyone and wants to be surrounded by people they know. They want people with whom they have built a bond of trust. It's all about relationships.

By the way, individual relationships should be 50/50 partnerships—i.e., both parties make an effort to nurture the friendship. If only one person is trying, then a balance will be lacking, and it will be a one-sided, dysfunctional relationship. You may find some people are difficult to build a relationship with. This happens. You can't win everyone's heart and mind, so don't kill yourself trying to make everyone happy.

Some people may not act very friendly if something tragic is going on in their personal life that they don't want to share with others. Give them space. If you don't really like someone or can't seem to get along at work, you still need to maintain a professional relationship. There is nothing to gain by alienating them. Be polite, friendly, and helpful. You never know what the future holds—their icy exterior could melt one day. Besides, you never know who could end up being your boss someday. Trust me on this one.

"Your reputation and integrity are everything.
Follow through on what you say you're going to do.
Your credibility can only be built over time,
and it is built from the history of your words and actions."
– Maria Razumich-Zec

HAVE INTEGRITY

Decorum, trust, and honesty are essential qualities needed to establish your credibility and integrity. In addition, you should always maintain your decorum when you are with people from work—even when socializing after work. It's a given you will inevitably have work friends that you may hang out with, but never embarrass yourself in front of someone who can make or break your career. You can't walk it back.

If you are at a work event or conference where alcohol is served, limit yourself to no more than <u>two drinks</u> for the entire evening. As a rule of thumb, your body can process about one drink per hour. (Ask your doctor about this one.) Let others make fools of themselves but not you. Successful people realize they are viewed under a microscope at all times, and any error in judgment will be seen and remembered. Your integrity is your *brand*. Be aware of how your actions could be perceived in public and maintain your composure.

Keep your promises. Your word has to mean something. Know that in order to maintain lasting relationships, having integrity is critical to your success and to building trust with others. People will find out if you don't keep your word. Be trust<u>worthy</u>.

Likewise, a big part of establishing integrity is **honesty**. If you never lie, you never have to remember what lies you told to cover your tracks. Likewise, understand that <u>maintaining</u> people's trust isn't nearly as difficult as <u>restoring</u> their trust. In short, do what you say you will do and keep your promises. If you can't deliver on a promise, then don't write checks with your mouth you cannot cash.

CHALLENGE THE STATUS QUO

If you accept things without question, you will greatly reduce your chances of distinguishing yourself from the pack. Everywhere I have worked, I have been able to improve processes and procedures. Often, when I questioned why things were done a certain way, I would get the blank look and cricket sound in the background. You need to look at how things are done with fresh eyes. In this way, you can come up with more efficient, effective ways to do things.

To illustrate my point, consider the story about the psychologists who were conducting an experiment involving five monkeys, a cage, a ladder, a banana, and a water hose. It begins with the psychologists setting up a big cage. Inside the cage, they hung a banana on a string and placed a ladder under it. Then they put five monkeys into the cage. Almost immediately, one of the monkeys started climbing the ladder to get the banana. Without delay, the psychologists hosed down all the monkeys with ice-cold water. When the next monkey tried to get the banana, the psychologists sprayed all the monkeys with ice-cold water again. After a while, whenever a monkey tried to climb the ladder, the other monkeys attacked him to prevent him from getting to the banana.

After this, the experimenters removed one monkey from the cage and replaced him with a new one. When the new monkey saw the banana and started to climb the stairs all the other monkeys beat him up. Next, the experimenters removed another of the four original monkeys and replaced him with another new one. When the second new monkey started climbing the ladder, it was attacked. The psychologists also noticed the <u>first new monkey</u> took part in this punishment—even though he had never been sprayed with water! The same thing happened when the third original monkey was replaced with a new one, then the fourth, then the fifth. Every time a new monkey touched the ladder, it was attacked by the other monkeys.

In the end, the monkeys that were beating up each other had no idea why they were not allowed to go after the banana or why they were beating up the newest monkey. Remember, all the original monkeys were replaced, so none of the remaining monkeys had ever been sprayed with the ice-cold water. A new "norm" had been established and no monkeys went after the banana. Why, you ask? Because "That's the way it's always been done around here."

The moral of this story is you don't have to accept things as they are. It's okay to respectfully challenge the status quo. It's smart to question "why" the team should keep adhering to an existing process—especially if the current process is problematic. While it's good to ask how the current process or procedure was created, be aware you could be asking the person who created it, so choose your words carefully.

To sell your idea, ask the person responsible for the process if they would consider another option. Suggest the team give it a trial run. Ask if the team would try the new process for a week and evaluate the results to see if it is more efficient/easier/faster. If, after a week, you all agree it's a better way to work and can quantify the benefit to the department . . . then you will adopt the new process going forward. (To avoid future confusion, be sure to document the new process and remove all obsolete versions.)

A word of caution here. Don't make this a daily thing within your work group, or they may perceive you as disruptive and not a team player. They may tire of what they interpret as constant complaining, and you will wear them out. Understand your team dynamics, watch their body language, and have the good sense to know when you might be pushing your luck. As a rule, people can only accept change in digestible, bite-sized chunks.

CONSTANTLY LEARN

According to the Pew Research Center, the average American reads five (5) books per year. Since graduating from high school, how many books have you read? How many books, trade publications, or magazine articles have you read in the last few months that are non-fiction? If it has been a while since you last read something to help you improve your career, you are falling behind. The level of effort you put into career development is comparable to how a professional athlete prepares in the sense that you are either getting *into shape* by doing the right exercises or you are *getting out of shape* by doing too little.

Don't let your competition outwork you. You need to continually exercise your mind and do the things you need to do to get to the next level. If you are not a Mensa genius or look like a European model, then <u>outworking</u> everyone can be your competitive advantage. Hard work and passion can beat untapped talent.

Think about that. If you work in an office setting and most of the employees have a high-school diploma, a few co-workers have an associate's degree, but one person is going to night school working on his or her bachelor's degree . . . who do you think is learning something new every day? All things being equal, who do you think will have the best chance to get ahead? If you invest in yourself and continually strive to improve your people skills and technical expertise, you will be a difference-maker, and people will notice.

Even after college, the most successful people still strive to take in new information all the time to maintain their edge. Unfortunately, I have seen too many people who thought once they earned their degree or certification they were through learning. They are wrong. Successful people remain students of their profession for life.

Constantly take in new information and learn from your experiences. You can also learn from your co-workers and your boss—both the good and the bad. For example, have you ever seen your boss say or do something you thought was wrong? Did you find yourself thinking, "If I am ever the boss, I will <u>never</u> do that?" Learning *what not to do* is learning too!

Top performers are never satisfied. Even after having earned a post-graduate degree and professional certifications, they continue to add knowledge to their mental toolbox. That's why it's so important to select a profession that's a labor of love—not something that bores you to tears. If you don't love (or at least like alot) what you do, you will find a million ways to avoid doing it.

PRODUCE RESULTS

On the job, you don't get points for participating—you get points for producing results. That doesn't mean you leave a string of dead bodies in your wake along the way either. When given a task or project to complete, make sure you understand exactly what you are being asked to do. It's a good practice to confirm you heard everything correctly and did not misinterpret instructions. I have been in situations where I thought I gave clear guidance to someone to produce a specific result, and the actual deliverable was different or did not have the level of detail I expected. If you are unclear, repeat the work instructions by paraphrasing what you heard back to your teacher/boss/spouse.

Some employers post employee performance, sales pipeline statistics, and department metrics in a central location for all to see.

Where do you want your name to be on the employee performance scorecard? At the top of the list with the best performers or at the bottom of the list?

If you are consistently at the bottom of the list, it is a safe bet your job could eventually be in jeopardy. For-profit businesses compete for the consumer dollar. The best businesses employ the top people to stay ahead, and there is constant pressure to perform. In a sense, free markets create a kind of economic Darwinism. Market leaders figure out how to be more efficient, improve results, and do more with less. As a result, managers are continually culling the herd of non-performers to improve overall performance. You will need to consistently produce results to remain part of the team because companies have short memories.

NEVER QUIT

It is easy to quit. You don't have to do anything but just give up. It requires no effort to throw a pity party and complain about how it's everyone else's fault. But guess what? You have to make your own luck. If it was easy, we would all be millionaires and retire by the age of twenty-five. But you know that success doesn't work that way. You will have to persevere when other people lose faith in themselves. If you really want to feel pride in yourself and your accomplishments, it will be because you overcame all odds and succeeded in spite of what life threw at you.

If you get a new boss at work, she will not be automatically compelled to promote you because you have worked there for X number of years. Don't depend on job tenure as your long-term strategy to climb the career ladder. People are naturally drawn to those who have self-confidence, are independent thinkers, and to those who are willing to take on responsibility. People who shrink from responsibility fade into the woodwork.

One of my best friends in the Army told me, "When you get knocked down, pick yourself up, brush yourself off . . . and continue with the mission." It was good advice then and still is today. If work or life gets you down, figure out a way to come back strong. Your response should be to make up for it by delivering a higher quality work product with the next project or task assigned to you. Pursue excellence in all that you do. If life gives you lemons, make lemonade! If you do that, no one can stop you. When things look their bleakest . . . when you feel your worst . . . by default, the next day will be better. The worst is be behind you.

"Never, never, never give up."
– Winston Churchill

Behaviors that Impede Success

In the last section, we looked at the behaviors that can help advance your career. Now, let's turn to behaviors that are career limiters. One example that may seem obvious, but I've seen it happen way too often, is being seen playing games on your smartphone, posting on social media, or shopping online when your boss or visiting executives are walking by your workstation. Do that in the break room or in private. And please don't compound the offense by trying to defend your actions. Enough said on that one, let's move on to other career killers.

In my past, a good practice I used to get to know my team better was to hold skip-level one-on-one meetings. In this case, I had managers reporting to me, and my managers had individual contributors reporting to them. (A skip-level 1:1 is a meeting between me and one of my manager's individual contributors.) Since I had over a hundred people in my department, I scheduled individual skip-level meetings with all of my reports. In our 1:1s, I asked a bunch of questions like how long had they been with the company, what their career goals were, where they were from, what keeps them coming back to work every day, and what kinds of changes they would like to see. One individual told me he'd been there four years and his career goal was to do as little as possible and get paid as much as possible. Wow! He said that out loud to me!

If you ever feel the urge to blurt out something like that, don't. Think it, but don't say it. That is the definition of tone deaf. In so many words, he just told me not to invest any energy into his career development because he doesn't really care about the company's goals, his teammates, or me. Got it. Thanks. Good talk!

Below are several more examples of what not to do. In general, know that management frowns upon the behaviors described here and repeating is asking for trouble.

MAKE EXCUSES

If you regularly blame others, your situation, your childhood, your parents, or anything else you can think of rather than being accountable for your words and deeds, then this is a behavior you need to examine more closely—and eliminate. If something you said or did caused a problem at work, you need to own it. It can be a tough pill for people to swallow when they have to admit they are wrong. Apologizing when you are wrong takes a measure of intestinal fortitude, but the alternative is toxic. If you have the courage to admit when you screw up, then people around you grant you one integrity credit. This may not let you off the hook for the mistake, but they will appreciate you are someone who has a moral compass and some personal honor, which are admirable traits.

When you admit your mistake to the person you have wronged, oftentimes this can diffuse the situation. I recall missing a business review deadline some time back, and my customer called me to meet him at his office to discuss it. I thought I was going to get read the riot act. When I got there, I could tell he was not happy, and he sharply asked me what happened. After a quick gulp to swallow my pride, I told him I screwed up . . . that I had made a mistake and had no excuse. He looked me straight in the eyes and said that was all he wanted to hear. He asked me what I was going to do to fix it, and we moved on. The lesson here is if you screw up—and we all do eventually—have the courage to 'fess up and face it.

SAY THAT'S NOT MY JOB

Another piece of advice is to never, ever, say "that's not my job" or "that's not in my job description." If your boss overhears you say that, his face will turn purple with anger. Companies are under immense pressure from global competition, which has caused them to operate with lean organizations and minimal headcount. In short, they have to do more with less. Gone are the days of having narrow, specialized job descriptions. Today, your job is pretty much to do whatever is needed to achieve the mission. Therefore, if you want to get ahead, you can't be limited by placing artificial constraints to doing what is required. You should have the mindset you will do whatever is needed—as long as it's legal and ethical—even if that means coming in early, working late, or over the weekend to complete a project on time.

Other defenses like, "I'm overworked so I couldn't complete the task you wanted me to do," are just excuses and don't hold water. Your boss will see through that and ask, "At what point did you know you were not going to be able to produce results?" and "When were you going to let me know about this issue?"

USE CONFUSION FOR SELF-DEFENSE

As a teenager in middle school or high school, you may have heard someone say "my dog ate my homework." Everybody really knows they just didn't do their homework. In the workplace, the equivalent is saying you didn't complete an assignment because you a) did not know what the boss wanted, b) misinterpreted what he said, or c) were unclear how he wanted something done. You may get away with this once or twice if you're a newbie, but when you are being paid to do a job, this excuse gets old quickly and is a fast way to get on the naughty list.

If you are unclear about an assignment or work task, it is *your* responsibility to ask questions. Even if you believe you are clear, it's still a good practice to paraphrase your boss's instructions back to him to show you understand what is being requested of you. If you miss a deadline, you may find out your bungle doesn't affect just you . . . it affects your whole team too. In the workplace, if you make it a practice of missing due dates regularly, it will damage your credibility. If you are unclear, ask clarifying questions.

BE NEGATIVE

When I used to deliver software training, there seemed to always be at least one Negative Nancy attending each session. She was like Glum from the old cartoon "Gulliver's Travels" and would (in so many words) say "It'll never work" or "It's hopeless" or "We're doomed." Eventually, I learned to overcome these objections by telling the naysayer to raise the issue with their boss. Still, it does get tiresome.

In some work groups, negativity is part of its culture, which can be poisonous. You can tell you are in a negative environment when you hear your co-workers (or even management) sharing negative thoughts about the company, its policies, or other co-workers. We are all a little guilty of griping on occasion because sometimes we need to let off a little steam. However, it's not acceptable to say hurtful things to others, to constantly be in sarcastic mode, or make cutting remarks about people in front of their co-workers. You can find these negative types talking in hushed tones in the break room, by the water cooler, or in the hallways. They gossip about how Annie's project is doomed to fail, how Daniel screwed up again, or that Trevor is so dumb and never does anything right. They talk about how insane this company policy is or how mean that boss is. This kind of talk is toxic, non-productive, and needs to be avoided.

Constant complaining in the workplace is detrimental to everyone's happiness. In addition, you don't want to be seen next to or with this crowd. If management observes you hanging out with negative people, you will be connected with them—a la guilt by association. If you play next to a mud puddle, you *will* get dirty.

UNDERMINE OTHERS TO GET AHEAD

Showing off or telling everyone how smart you are exposes a character flaw that tells others you are insecure or hiding something. It makes people think you believe you are superior to them. What's worse, I've seen extreme cases where a person told blatant falsehoods about a rival she was competing with for a promotion. That is not acceptable. Other tactics used by these Machiavellian personality types include belittling someone in front of their peers in an attempt to bully and embarrass them. It is disturbing to see someone would be so immoral as to purposely hurt someone else.

Beware of the passive-aggressive version of this. You may be in a meeting and observe one person consistently cutting off others before they can complete their sentences. They know this is disrespectful, but when challenged, they will feign surprise and offer an insincere apology. Another way they try to undermine others is to withhold vital information rather than confront someone or have an honest debate.

Avoid these types of behaviors. Make sure the person staring back at you in the mirror is someone who is principled, has integrity, and genuinely cares about others.

PLAY THE VICTIM

Customarily, if you want to get ahead, you need to outperform your peers. You will have to work smarter, faster, and produce higher-quality output. Oftentimes, overachieving will result in positive recognition for doing a good job. If not, you need to take matters into your own hands. Don't brood about it. I can't recall anyone ever getting promoted because they moped around the office all day. If things aren't going your way at work, figure out a way to change it. If you were passed over for a promotion, find out why and figure out what you need to do to be *promotable*.

For those who work in an office environment, schedule a regular one-on-one with your direct supervisor. Having a weekly (or at least bi-weekly) 1:1 is the best way to keep your boss up to date about what you are doing. You can use this time to align your priorities with him or her. It's an opportunity to pitch your proposal on how to improve sales or reduce cost. A regular a 1:1 is also a good way to keep your boss informed about what's going in his or her department. Your boss needs someone they can trust, someone who has a finger on the pulse of the team to let them know how team morale is, or be a sounding board for their ideas.

Don't wait for the mountain to come to you. Take the initiative and reach out to your boss to build a positive working relationship and to show you have ambition. You don't have to be besties, but you do have to maintain a professional relationship, communicate regularly, and get along.

PROCRASTINATE

Procrastination is a roadblock to success. If you put something off that you know you're supposed to do by a certain deadline, you will feel ashamed if you miss it. One big reason people procrastinate is they are afraid of failure. In order to realize your potential, you will need to face your fear. You can overcome procrastination if you understand what is stopping you from doing the right thing. The most common excuses of why people procrastinate are doubt about their ability to do the work well, a lack of ambition, or not liking their job.

To help frame this, let's discuss the consequences of procrastination. I have seen it up close and personal. Years ago, a family member told me he wanted to go back to college. We were both in our twenties, but I was single with no kids and he was married with two children. He started out by taking two night classes at a local community college. He got an A and a B! Clearly, he had the intelligence and capacity to learn. But then he stopped.

In my family member's case, he explained he quit because it was too hard to go to school with kids. He said he would go back later when his kids were bigger. While I can appreciate how hard it is to go to college with children, he later conceded that he wished he would've continued taking at least one class at a time until he finished.

The lesson to be learned is don't put off doing what you need to do to fulfill your dreams. Time is not your friend. Once you stop pursuing your dream and lose momentum, it's harder to re-start the process. In your idle time, you start making excuses like "I'm just putting my goals on pause for a while." Even though you know in your heart what the right thing to do is, you stray from the path that you know will take you where you want to go.

On the other hand, when you maintain the discipline to forge ahead and do what is needed, you feel a sense of accomplishment.

You are proud of yourself, and you should be. You have earned that right. Remember what we discussed in Chapter 1; you owe it to your family to do as much as you possibly can to provide a better life for them. It takes sacrifice, but you owe it to yourself, too, to find a rewarding and fulfilling career.

To keep your energy going, it may help to bribe yourself with a nice reward once in a while—especially if you complete a task you dread doing. For me, if I finished an assignment on time, I would treat myself to an ice cream cone, the latest car magazine, or a drive up north for the weekend to visit friends. Do what you must do to complete the mission. Rewarding yourself for doing the right things along the way is perfectly acceptable.

EXPECT QUICK SUCCESS

I have seen new hires come in and expect immediate success. Research on Millennials claim they expect a promotion every one to two years and raises, recognition, and bonuses to be awarded more than once a year. This may be true for the top 5 percent of workers, but it is not the norm. In your career, you will inevitably encounter a few of the anointed ones who believe they will achieve grand success. While believing in yourself isn't a bad thing, it is impractical to think you will advance up the career ladder without having to pay your dues.

Of course, there are exceptions. Some people do advance quicker than others, but it is usually because they work hard, are smarter than the average bear, have great social skills, are charming . . . or all of the above. However, they are the exception, not the rule.

For those who are counting on quick success, you would do well to temper your expectations a little. I know I started out this book by asking you to dream big, but I didn't say dream big and you will get everything yesterday. It's a process. The things in life worth having and the things you appreciate most are the things you had to work hard for. For 99 percent of us, success doesn't come overnight—it is earned. Be at peace with that.

ACCEPT DEFEAT

Life has a (not so) funny way of finding ways to test your will. As you strive to make a better life for yourself, you will be challenged. You may find yourself having to pay unplanned car repair expenses when your car won't start, so you borrow your cousin's Camaro to get to night school in the winter, and on your way, a Jeep 4x4 starts spinning out of control on the icy road and crashes into your cousin's car . . . that you were driving. Of course, your cousin won't have collision insurance either. (That never happened to me.) For you, maybe it's a professor who doesn't like you because you look exactly like the boy who stole his high-school sweetheart. Challenges like these can come from anywhere at the most unexpected and least appreciated times. This is life.

If you are breathing, you are not defeated. Why? Because when you feel so bad you think you can't possibly feel any worse, then the next day is—by default—better! When you reach rock bottom, logic dictates you will bounce upward. Take advantage of that momentum. Muster the COURAGE to continue. This doesn't mean you will never be afraid. In fact, it is quite the opposite. Everyone experiences doubt—moments of weakness.

"Courage: the mental or moral strength to venture, persevere, and withstand danger, fear, or difficulty."
– Merriam-Webster

I heard Randi Zuckerberg speak once at a conference. She was telling the story about when her brother asked her to take over marketing at Facebook. She was afraid. She didn't think she could do it. She told herself she didn't have the experience to take on such a big job. Yet, her brother was asking, so she did it. At this point in the story, she laughed and told the audience she had no choice but to forge ahead! She also shared her secret . . . *Fake it until you make it.*

The moral of her story is there will be times in your life where you need to rally up some intestinal fortitude and forge ahead. What's the worst that could happen? You might make mistakes. We all do. But if you learn from your mistakes, there's a good chance you will get through it and be all the better for it. Other people have undertaken great challenges with little or no prior training or experience. They were probably afraid, just like you. The real question to ask is "Why can't you do it too?" Why not you?

9 – MASTER YOUR PROFESSION

"The quality of a person's life is in direct proportion to their commitment to excellence, regardless of their chosen field of endeavor."
– Vince Lombardi

Back when I was going to college (for the second time around) and found myself struggling to get A's, in my mind, I thought I was doing all the right things. I went to class, took notes, read the textbook, and tried to remember all the material. The night before the big exam, I would cram and try to memorize everything that was going to be covered.

For most eighteen-year-olds starting college, all they really only need to worry about is going to class and keeping up with their homework. They are intelligent and have great short-term memories. They can breeze through tests, get great grades, and graduate with honors. In my case, I had just gotten out of the military and was finally keeping a promise to myself to return to school to earn a bachelor's degree. I had a full-time day job and attended college at night. On top of that, I put a lot of pressure on myself to catch up with my peers and believed I needed top grades to land a good job and, eventually, be accepted to graduate school.

For the classes in my major, I had no problem getting good grades. Those were the classes that interested me. However, I wasn't doing as well in classes that were required as part of the curriculum. One night, I was studying late into the night and, after reading the same sentence for goodness knows how many times, it hit me. I asked myself "Why don't I actually *try to learn* about the subject instead of just memorizing everything?" If I was to get a well-rounded education, I needed to learn about a wider range of topics than just the technical courses in my major. Otherwise, I thought, I would just be getting *trained*—not educated. For me, that was my little epiphany.

After that, I went to class with a new attitude. I actively listened to what the professor was teaching. I told myself this was his field of specialty and he was an expert. I tried to identify with why he was so passionate about the topic. I pictured myself in a social setting where I might find myself speaking with someone on the subject and wondered how the exchange might go. I had a choice. I could be oblivious when someone raises the topic, or I can learn enough to speak with some intelligence and perhaps connect with that person. I felt renewed. I had a better outlook about school after that. I finally realized the point of going to school was to teach you *how to learn*!

"A man cannot understand the art he is studying
if he only looks for the end result
without taking the time to delve deeply
into the reasoning of the study."
– Miyamoto Musashi

BE A JEDI MASTER

So how does becoming a Jedi relate to work? You may find yourself having to perform tasks you find incredibly boring but still need to pay attention to detail. Inevitably, you will have to attend meetings whose agenda covers topics you think don't really impact you. This is when you need to restrain yourself from drifting off into some daydream, a la Walter Mitty. At work, it matters how others perceive you. Will they see someone who is engaged and committed to the team? Or will your body language suggest you don't care and have checked out?

Doing the work that interests you most isn't the problem. It's everything else that comes along with it. No detail is too small if you are going to master your profession. You need to learn what the next person does . . . the one who is providing inputs that trigger you to perform your job. Understand how your work output affects the people who use your output as their input. In short, you need to learn the whole business to master your profession. Otherwise, you are just mastering discrete tasks assigned to you. You will be an order taker.

Let's use a specific example to show what it means to master your profession. Imagine you are an automotive product engineer responsible for the armrest on the inner door panel for a next-generation pickup truck. Upon getting the assignment, you should be asking questions like:

1. How does my part fit with the overall aesthetics of the interior door panel assembly?
2. What materials are related components made of?
3. Will temperature changes affect how parts fit together and affect durability, buzz squeak, or rattle?
4. How does the tactile feel of the materials used compare to your competitors?
5. How does the design meet the ergonomics of the cabin?
6. How can it be efficiently manufactured?
7. How should it be installed on the assembly line? In house or outsourced as a modular assembly supplied and installed by the vendor?
8. How easily can it be replaced in case of part failure or an accident?

If you know the answers to all these questions, it's a good start. These initial discoveries are only the outer layer of the onion. You have to be honest with yourself and ask if you are "all in" with mastering your profession. Have you visited the supplier's facilities?

Toured their plants? Are you engaged with your boss and your team? This is all about you and your level of emotional commitment to the organization and its goals.

Assuming you are in a job you like—or better yet, doing something you love—you should realize mastering your profession is more than learning to be technically competent at repeatable tasks. It is becoming aware of everything and everybody connected with what you do. It is learning the business and the industry you are in. It is knowing how the business processes run upstream from your piece of the puzzle and how what you do affects the downstream activity chain. Likewise, you should continually find innovative ways to do your job better.

Become an EXPERT at what you do. This takes time and acceptance of the fact that you can't do it alone. You need to develop relationships with your circle of like-minded colleagues who are equally committed to excellence. If you develop relationships, you can share the ideas and knowledge you have learned with others.

SHARE KNOWLEDGE

If you develop a way to improve a business process, document it so the organization can duplicate good practices (and you won't have to re-invent the wheel next time you are assigned a similar project). Documenting what you know enables the company and more junior co-workers to benefit from what you have learned.

Don't be a knowledge hoarder. Withholding knowledge so nobody else will know what you know does NOT boost your job security. It does quite the opposite. In my career, I have seen cases where workers refused to share what they knew and then found themselves being put in a corner with the light on dim (career-wise). If you don't share what you know so others can learn how to do your job, you may find yourself stuck in the same position forever instead of moving up. If you refuse to play well with others, people who are more collaborative and better communicators will pass you by. So share what you know with your co-workers. You're the idea-person. You will never have a shortage of new ideas.

If you are naturally introverted, make a sincere effort to interact with other carbon-based life forms. Very few occupations allow you to lock yourself in a bubble and thrive (except maybe for actuaries and computer programmers). If you don't share what you know so others can grow, you are being inefficient because those who follow you will have to re-discover how to perform tasks you've already figured out.

Instead, why don't you take credit for solving the puzzle once, share that knowledge, and enable everybody who follows to maintain the standard. For recurring, low-risk tasks, you can develop an SOP (Standard Operating Procedure) so your team can produce repeatable, high-quality work products or services. Your boss will notice too. Accomplishments like that will increase your chances of advancing up the ladder. People who master their profession can teach and develop others. In fact, I have found when you teach others, you learn your job even better, and that's when you truly become a professional.

"The secret of change is to focus all of your energy,
not on fighting the old but on building the new."
– Dan Millman

ACCEPT CHANGE

Over time, you will find advances in technology, how businesses compete, trends in management practices, and people's work styles will change. In your career, you will see company executives—and your bosses—come and go. It is inevitable. The only guarantee in life is *things will change*, so you might as well be flexible and embrace change.

If a new process or change disrupts your area at work, don't let it throw you off your game. If someone above your pay grade introduces a new procedure or form to fill out, don't let it get to you. Give them the benefit of the doubt. Assume there was a well-thought-out reason for changing the old process.

Someday, you may become a boss, and it's very likely you will want to improve a policy, process, or procedure. In your mind, you would only propose changes to increase sales, lower cost, or improve safety, right? The last thing you'd want to do is to pile on some administrative burden that adds no value. Conversely, assume the intentions of your boss or organization are the same. Leaders are constantly striving to find ways to be more productive, more efficient, and more profitable. If you are selected to lead a project one day, you will be faced with introducing and managing change within your organization.

MANAGE CHANGE

So how do you manage change? Let's assume you are leading a project at work. The project will modify how people use some system. Knowing human nature, you anticipate there will be resistance to change, so a top-down approach is the best way to get people on board with the program. If senior leadership supports the change, your chances are greatly improved. Specifically, seek the support of someone in upper management who will agree to be the project or business sponsor. Ask him to say a few words at the kickoff meeting that includes the leaders of the departments this project will be affecting. When it's your turn to speak, be enthusiastic. Start with something like:

> I've got great news! We listened to your suggestions on how to improve the widget manufacturing process. In fact, some of you in the room helped us pilot the solution. Based on your input, we were able to get leadership buy-in to streamline how we make widgets. The new process has fewer steps, is safer for our assembly workers, and the process has 30 percent faster throughput. Up on the screen now is the project implementation timeline. We plan to start the project . . ."

PERCEPTION IS REALITY

Perception is reality, so why not manage perception. If you are enthusiastic about your project and inclusive, it becomes EVERYONE's project, not just yours. If you got valuable input from some of the people in the room, recognize them. For the most part, people love to be praised. Cover why the project was initiated, clarify project scope (as well as what is out of scope), solution benefits, and project timeline, and your communication and change management plan is to ensure the transition goes as smooth as possible.

The more you include the people who are impacted by your project, the more people will be on board. It is better to over-communicate than to under-communicate when managing change. After all, you want to deliver goodness FOR people, not TO people.

Ask for their suggestions on how to improve the process or tighten the requirements. Give a little . . . incorporate their feedback wherever possible. People are less resistant to something that is partly their idea. The more you involve them early on, the more likely you will have their support at and after you go live.

Lastly, when walking from your work space to another part of the building, walk with a purpose. Don't lollygag from here to there like you've nowhere to be and are just wasting time. Have the kind of serious expression on your face like you're on a mission. Look and act the part and you'll be perceived as someone who needs to be taken seriously.

THE CHANGE CYCLE

When planning a project, I learned long ago it is MORE IMPORTANT to manage the PEOPLE CHANGE aspect than the technical part. You can have the best solution in the world, but if no one knows about it, the right people don't sign off on the changes, or key people don't like the colors used on the web site, you are at risk of having a failed implementation. It's worth repeating, communicate early and often.

Over the years, I noticed there really isn't a whole lot that separates the organizational change management process from the **Grief Cycle**—i.e., shock/denial, anger, depression, negotiation, and finally, acceptance. You can use this to your advantage.

Shock is how most people react when a new change is brought up for the first time. People express *denial* when they want to continue to do their job the way they always have and hope you'll just go away. They think, "I've worked here twenty years and seen folks like you come and go. I'll just wait it out and one day will all be rid of you too."

Anger and *depression* are self-explanatory, and I've seen people behave pretty poorly when forced to change how they work. They sulk, mope around the office, and pick arguments over little things. People start to turn the corner in the *negotiation* phase. This is when you can start hammering out the details of how the changes will apply to their work and how best to navigate through the objections they raise. Here, they realize the train is coming, and they need to get on board or get run over or left behind. *Acceptance* is when everyone finally comes to terms with what shall become the new normal.

Again, the more lead-time you give people to process changes in their mind ... the more you deliver regular, consistent communication ... the more likely you will convince them to go along with the changes you are proposing. Be upbeat and emphasize the benefits of the project and how implementing this solution helps the company achieve its goals. Be patient and remember the hardest part about managing resistance to change is always the people.

Don't Get Ahead of the Organization

Patience is a virtue, right? It is wise to not get overly enthusiastic about an idea and become impatient if it doesn't happen yesterday. We just discussed at length that the "people" part of *change* is the hardest part when implementing new ideas. If you have a great idea, understand you won't be successful if you try to implement a new change too fast—before you have allowed people enough time to go through the Grief Cycle.

If you are overzealous and rush blindly ahead, you could end up like a young antelope in the Serengeti sprinting haphazardly ahead of the herd. If you are smart, you will quickly realize you are out on your own, lose steam, and drift back to the rest of the team. If you get too far ahead of the herd, there will be no one out there to protect you. You will be vulnerable to attack and accused of not being a team player. Be wary of trying to go faster than your boss or your organization's ability to process change.

My advice when trying to implement a change is to first make sure you get everyone involved who has a stake in the implementation of your idea. Float the concept with them early on in the process. Socialize your idea with your boss so he can have your back. Involve the people who will be impacted by your project and ask for their input. Ask your boss who else may be impacted and ask if he would speak with them about your idea to get their support too. You will discover people in different roles will offer perspectives you did not think of, which can further help you avoid landmines on your way to delivering your project.

> *"The customer isn't always right,*
> *but they are still the customer."*
> *– Jean-Claude Eclairé*

PROVIDE GREAT CUSTOMER SERVICE

A hilarious commercial I saw years ago illustrates the epitome of poor customer service. Imagine this. You are driving in the pouring rain and need to find a gas station because your tank is almost empty. Through the pouring rain, you see a big sign that says "Full Service" on one row of pumps, so you pull up next to the sign. As you stop, you see a lone attendant inside hurriedly putting on his yellow rain slicker and fisherman's hat and run toward you. You're smiling to yourself because you think you're getting the full-service treatment. To your horror, the attendant runs past your car, flips the sign to "Self-Serve," and runs back into the station. The commercial ends with the camera panning from the shocked look on your face and the narrator saying, "Did you ever get the feeling they quit trying?"

In every profession, your customer service skills will make or break your career. To help you with this concept, think of every interaction you have with every customer, every manager, and every co-worker as an **audition**. People will remember with uncanny accuracy how you treated them five years ago. Do you recall our discussion about your *brand*? This is one of the ways you create and maintain your brand.

It may help to think of yourself as a franchise and everyone is your customer—for the rest of your life. Your brand and reputation are your greatest assets. What you learn, the skills you possess, and how well you can apply them will determine (or limit) your level of success. The customer service part is how well you deliver your franchise services to others.

If you work in a retail clothing store, it's easy to understand that the patrons who walk through the front door are your "external" paying customers. As a sales clerk, it is your job to meet their needs, but you will both benefit if you make the transaction the most pleasant experience possible. When you welcome them to your store, accompany your greeting with a big smile. It's amazing how many people will smile back. In fact, a smile can disarm folks who may have been having a bad day—that is until they met you.

Introduce yourself and ask for the customer's name. Be sure to listen well so you can remember. It helps to use their name in your next few sentences. People love the sound of their own name! If it is an unusual name, ask how it is spelled and compliment them on how unique or nice it is. Observe everything about your customer, such as what clothes they are wearing, what they are carrying, who is with them, etc. Make small talk such as, "Wow, you've got the whole family with you today!" or "Are you shopping for a special occasion?" Ask how the person's day is going so far and get the customer to talk about herself. The more you learn about your customer, the better you can meet their needs.

After the purchase, congratulate your customer on making such a smart choice. People want to feel good when they make a purchasing decision—especially if it was on sale. Make it easy for your customer to brag to their friends about how you complimented them on getting such a great deal. If you want to build a book of repeat clientele, invite them back. Give them a business card if you have one, and tell them to ask for you the next time they come back.

DAMAGE CONTROL

Customer Service also includes how well you solve your customer's problems when things go wrong. For example, if a customer approaches you to complain about an experience she had with your company, make sure you listen attentively to the issue. You are representing your organization and, as such, are its representative. Always apologize for the inconvenience the issue has caused. If the customer is upset, the most important thing you should do at this point is to agree with them—even if you know she is wrong. If you agree, your chances increase you will be able to defuse the situation. When dealing with an irate customer, you can respond with something like this:

> *My apologies, Mrs. Bailey. If I were in your situation, I would feel the same way you do. I feel terrible about this. Thank you for bringing this to my attention. What can I do to make this right?"*

Think about this statement. Do you want to spend your time "winning" the argument and losing a customer? Or is it better to agree with them and work it out? Being agreeable with the customer increases your chances of keeping them as a customer. You may even find she is willing to recommend a more reasonable solution than you would have suggested.

However you work out the resolution, consider this encounter is a test of whether you want to retain or lose a customer—forever. If you work in the service industry, I recommend you read *Customers for Life: How to Turn That One-Time Buyer into a Lifetime Customer* by Carl Sewell. It's a great read. You can get through it in a day, and it will stick with you always. Carl's premise is simple. If the average customer spends $1,700 per year in clothes, over fifty years, that makes a grand total of $85,000. So why not refund or exchange the $35 pair of pants with the obviously defective stitching? Isn't a $35 refund worth $85,000 in sales over their lifetime?

It pays to provide great customer service.

10 – Making Your Boss Successful

"The fundamental rule of employment:
You are there to make your manager successful."
– Lea McLeod

Many new entrants to the workforce believe if they work hard and produce quality results, they will be successful. The sad truth is working hard, being punctual, and taking pride in the quality of your work isn't enough to get ahead. In most cases, hard work alone won't get you the promotion you are hoping for. Showing up on time and putting in an acceptable level of effort is expected.

The one person who has the biggest influence in determining whether your career stalls or you get promoted is your boss. Hence, your real mission is to make your boss happy (as well as complete all the duties in your job description). Yes, you read that correctly. If your boss isn't happy with you, feels like he isn't kept informed, or has a hard time dealing with you . . . then your upward mobility will be put on pause.

To get ahead, you will need to help your boss achieve his personal and professional goals. After all, he has control over how you are rated in your performance reviews, decides how much you should get for a raise, and recommends who should get the next promotion. In this chapter, I share some essential dos and don'ts that can help you develop a positive working relationship with your boss and help him succeed—so you can too.

BE EASY TO WORK WITH

Step outside yourself and see yourself from other people's point of view. How easy are you to work with? What do you think your co-workers would say if they're asked that question? What would your boss say? Do you get to work early every day and take the initiative to get things rolling before he comes in? Or does he see you sitting around drinking coffee . . . waiting to be told what to do? If he has to prod you to get started every morning, it will get tiring. Bosses like self-starters. They don't like having to pull someone's teeth just to get people to do their job. Then again, if you make an effort to arrive early, learn your job, take the initiative to ask questions so you completely understand what the mission is, and do it without having to be told . . . you are probably someone who is easy to work with.

Whenever you meet someone new, do you introduce yourself? Create a network of support where you work. Make friends within and outside your department. Let people know they can contact you if they ever need anything from you or your department. Build strong working relationships. If you help them with something important to them, they may tell everybody what a great team player you are. Your reputation will begin to take shape. This will also benefit you whenever you ask for a return favor. When someone helps you or teaches you something new, show sincere appreciation so they will feel valued. If you do this, they'll be more apt to help you next time too.

In meetings, be willing to participate when you believe you can offer value. If you are still new or don't have deep expertise on a topic being discussed, sometimes asking a question about the big elephant in the room can be an ice breaker. Besides, being new usually gets you a free pass for asking questions and compels everyone else to have to address it. The more you participate, the more people will recognize you as someone who's engaged and part of the team.

KEEP YOUR BOSS INFORMED

If your boss doesn't know where you are, what you are working on, or hasn't been updated on what progress you've made on an important project, he will feel like you are not keeping him informed. Along the same lines, never allow your boss to be blindsided. Bosses don't like surprises—and surprises at work are usually bad. If he attends a meeting and his boss asks about a high-risk situation on the project you are working on, he will be unprepared to respond if you haven't updated him. It could jeopardize his credibility with his peers. Being blindsided creates man-made drama that usually results in more work . . . such as lessons-learned exercises, root-cause analysis, detailed forensic reports, and superfluous corrective actions that can be a waste of everybody's time.

Your boss wants to be successful, just like you do, so keep him informed. Let him know what you are doing. Help him get what he needs to be successful. In most cases, I think you'll find he'll help you in return.

Getting ahead is doing what it takes to get the job done well. It is the extra effort that stands out from your peers. I've mentioned this earlier, but creating Standard Operating Procedures (SOP) to document what you are doing enables you to produce repeatable, high-quality work. It shows you have leadership qualities. Your boss will notice you took the initiative without having to be told to do it. Now he can show this documentation to his boss, which leads to getting some positive exposure with leadership. Your boss may even earn some brownie points for "developing" you. Either way, he'll know who did this, and you will be thought of as a valued asset.

As I mentioned earlier, you should schedule regular one-on-one meetings with your boss. Don't wait for your boss to schedule this—take the initiative. Not every boss has a collaborative management style. Use this time to keep him informed about projects or tasks you are working on. Have an agenda or list of discussion items prepared beforehand that includes what ideas you have, any project issues or risks you need help with . . . and be sure to add what your recommendations are to demonstrate you are a problem-solver. This is also a perfect time to cover any personal issues such as needing time off for a dentist appointment scheduled two weeks from now. Your boss will be impressed to find you are a planner, are well organized, and someone who gets things done. Being aligned with your boss also helps diffuse unnecessary drama, such as the case when someone misstates an important fact about a project you're working on. If your boss is well informed, he is able to nip rumors in the bud.

DON'T BE ARGUMENTATIVE

If you second-guess your boss or constantly question why he is asking you to do something, you are hurting your upward mobility. If you do it often enough, he will start avoiding you because you drain his energy. If you feel you must contradict others to prove you are right, you need to cease that behavior right now. Besides, there are usually two losers to every argument—especially if you are trying to grind your superiority into a co-worker. Hence the saying, "A man convinced against his will is of the same opinion still."

People who are argumentative make themselves vulnerable, often without knowing it. Consider a scenario where you work for a publicly traded company and the analysts report poor financial performance for the quarter. Senior leadership may be compelled to respond by cutting operating expenses. Sometimes, this means selling off a subsidiary to generate cash. However, more often than not, this means laying off some percentage of their workforce. If your leadership has some discretion as to *how* to trim the fat in their department, they will likely target the poor performers and complainers to be downsized first. Don't be that person.

BOSSES PLAY FAVORITES

Regardless of whether they want to admit it or not, bosses do have favorites and treat their most valued employees better than the rest. These *teacher's pets* get promoted first, receive the best assignments, and are awarded the biggest raises. Bosses prefer the employees who work the hardest, are self-starters, and who are pleasant to be around. They value high performers who propose solutions as opposed to poor performers who bring problems to their boss's attention without any recommendation on how to fix things. Poor performers play the victim card and grumble about everything that is wrong with the company or how some policy isn't fair. Don't get twisted around the axle about whether something is fair or not. Life isn't fair. Learn to find ways to get over it and get with the program.

Now for some good news. *The Employee Engagement Group* conducted a study, and their results suggest seven out of ten employees are disengaged or actively disengaged on the job. That means only 30 percent of the workforce is going above and beyond the call of duty to make the company (and themselves) successful. Only 30 percent are engaged and committed to being a high performer. In a self-serving sort of way, you can view this as working to your benefit. If you are in the thirtieth percentile, you can be the cream of the crop.

ALL bosses play favorites. If you want to be one of their favorites, consider adopting some of the following habits:

- Take on projects over and above your normally assigned duties.
- Consistently complete assignments/projects/tasks on time.
- Complete assignments with a high degree of quality, without rework.
- Collaborate and get along well with co-workers.
- Keep everyone informed on progress—both good news and bad.

Regarding the last bullet, bad news does not get better with age. The sooner you let your boss know if something goes wrong, the sooner you can figure out a corrective action to get back on track. Remember, your Number One job is to make your boss look good.

A final note on the topic . . . I understand it's risky putting your future in the hands of a boss who *may* or *may not* have your best interests at heart. You can't control anyone but yourself, so do your part. Ask yourself what type of employee you are going to be. Are you going to be someone who is easy to work with, doesn't criticize, and doesn't complain . . . just consistently produces quality work with no drama? Are you going to be the great teammate? In the Army, we used to say you are either a HELP or a HINDRANCE. It does you no good to swim against the current, so you might as well help.

Types of Bosses

As an employee, you work for someone else—i.e., you don't own your own business and are not independently wealthy. If you think about it, you spend about half your waking hours between Monday and Friday with the same group of co-workers and bosses. If you are fortunate, you have a great boss who is a visionary, a great teacher, and a mentor who values you as a person. Your boss has a vested interest in actively helping you succeed.

On the other hand, some of you are not always so lucky. Not all bosses have gone through the ACME, Inc. *How to be a Great Leader* boot camp. Remember the employee engagement research that says only 30 percent of employees are actively engaged? This also applies to bosses. Unfortunately, a bad boss can make your work life very difficult.

Do you have a great boss? Have you ever had a bad boss? Let's examine the types of bosses you will likely encounter at different times in your career.

THE NEW BOSS

Sometimes, a bad boss is simply one who was recently promoted and is a first-time manager. Regrettably, most people get promoted because they were a good accountant, nurse, technician, or engineer. Being technically proficient does not automatically qualify you to be a good boss.

Besides, being a manager, supervisor, or foreman is a *different* job than being an individual contributor. While a manager's technical skills help them understand what their employees' jobs are and provide a foundation of industry knowledge, the competencies a good manager must possess are different than those of an individual contributor. Furthermore, new managers are not divinely inspired. It takes training, willingness, dedication, and experience to become a good manager. Essential skills to be a good boss include effective communication skills, an ability to build teams, understanding how to handle conflict, situational leadership, planning, and organizational skills. In short, they must have people management skills. The last time I looked, they don't teach that in engineering, fine arts, or healthcare programs.

Management is a different job. If you get a new boss who was recently promoted and a first-time manager, you may need to practice some patience while they learn their job. If you're lucky, you may get a new boss who was mentored by a good manager before getting promoted. He might be a great people person and a consensus builder. If your new boss is less experienced, you can make yourself indispensable by offering to do everything you can to help him or her be successful in the new role.

> *"Never lose sight of the fact that the most important yardstick of your success will be how you treat people —your family, friends, and coworkers, and even strangers you meet along the way."*
> *– Barbara Bush, Former First Lady, US*

BAD BOSS TYPES

Several studies claim the number one reason employees quit their jobs is because of a bad boss. Hence the phrase "People leave managers, not companies." This section outlines some behaviors that indicate someone may be a bad boss. For example, some bosses believe in ruling by decibel level. They try to intimidate people and bully their team. Maybe they were former military and used to having people follow their orders without question. Perhaps they are overcompensating to hide their insecurity or afraid someone might challenge their authority. In their previous job, they may have been ostracized and publicly humiliated by their boss and believe this is how the cold, cruel world works. Other more insidious types pit employees against each other in an effort to keep everyone off balance so they won't come after their job.

Then there is the *laissez-faire* boss. These boss types basically leave everyone alone and let their team figure things out on their own. Their office door is usually closed, or they aren't in the office at all. Perhaps they're timid or think everyone already knows how to do their job. This is fine until something inevitably goes wrong. The laissez-faire boss usually lacks the strength of character to deal with the issue. Confrontation isn't in their toolkit. They simply don't want to have the hard conversation. This becomes problematic because they avoid conflict to the point where—instead of addressing what was a minor issue—now it has become a huge problem. When they are finally forced to take action, it is more severe than what would have been needed if they would have taken immediate action.

Coping techniques can help you deal with bad bosses. For instance, try to find out what they want or what motivates them. If they are disorganized, help them be organized. If they are not good communicators, offer to be the one to talk to the team. If they do something that troubles you, have the courage to tell them how you feel. Give your boss a chance to fix it.

My aim in calling out these different types of bad bosses is to raise awareness in case you find yourself in that kind of a situation. If you spot one of these boss types during the interview process, you will have to incorporate it into your decision-making process. Suffice it to say, bad bosses generally don't last too long. In the end, they either improve how they treat people or are promoted to customer. Until then, try your best not to take it personally, remain confident in yourself, and know that this, too, shall pass.

If you find yourself in a situation with a bad boss who is behaving in a manner that is unprofessional or unfair to you, I recommend you have a respectful conversation where you tell your boss how you feel about certain behaviors. Don't make it personal. If that doesn't resolve your problem, make an appointment to consult with your Human Resources or Ethics representative to get their advice. It's their job to protect the company and you. Personally, I seek all other options before escalating it to HR.

"People don't care how much you know
until they know how much you care."
— Theodore Roosevelt

THE GOOD BOSS

During the interview process, remember, YOU are interviewing your future boss and the company too. Assuming you applied for a position in the field you want to pursue, you should also be looking for an organization that is a good fit with your personality, work style, and career goals. If you find the hiring manager seems to be the type of boss you can work for and the company culture is consistent with your values, your decision just became a lot easier.

When you consider the qualities of the good boss, you will find he cares about the employees under his charge. He often singles out people to recognize them for a job well done. He has a clear vision— is passionate about what he does—and is a decision maker. The good boss knows one of his greatest responsibilities is to develop his people and to lift them up. He is approachable and a good communicator. He empowers employees and treats them like professionals. The work environment is based on integrity and trust, which fosters a culture where people are treated fairly and there is a work-life balance. As a result, the culture becomes self-policing because employees hold themselves and their colleagues accountable.

Earlier, I mentioned employees join companies but leave bad bosses. While that may be true, most people can't just quit their job because they get off on the wrong foot with their new boss. To an extent, you can influence the relationship you have with your boss. As you get to know him, encourage and reward the positive behaviors described in this section. If you observe him giving someone praise for a job well done, let him know you appreciate him recognizing the efforts of others and how much it means to the team when he does that. In fact, you should also recognize others and raise awareness of your co-workers' contributions to your boss. Good news is *news*, too, and not enough good news seems to get around. If done well, employee recognition can be infectious. Others will appreciate you praising their work and will be more likely to reciprocate in kind when they observe you doing a good job.

Managing Up

Early in my career, I believed if I came to work on time, worked hard, and was a good person . . . that I would move up the ladder. It would be auto-magic! I assumed my boss would just notice. The older I got, the more I learned that my co-workers and friends felt this way about their careers too. This formula may work for you if you are fortunate enough to have one of the enlightened bosses who believe in the importance of developing their people.

As an employee, you have an obligation to put in an honest day's work for an honest day's pay. You should strive to be punctual, reliable, trustworthy, and produce high-quality work, product, or service. Bosses are held to a higher standard. From an employee's perspective, a good boss helps the team develop their talents, identify opportunities for career growth, and create an engaging work environment. From the company's viewpoint, bosses must do all the above plus establish clear performance standards, accomplish all of their goals, and complete all of the administrative overhead associated with being a manager.

In the report *The State of the American Manager*, Gallup claims only 18 percent of managers were rated with having "high talent" for leadership skills. Key attributes for high talent were the ability to encourage accountability, motivate workers, and build relationships with their teams. Their findings go on the say that 36 percent of managers and executives are <u>engaged</u>, 51 percent are <u>not engaged</u>, and another 14 percent are actively <u>disengaged</u>. Using this research as a basis, my unscientific method of guestimating the ratio between the "good" bosses versus bosses who are "not good" is 36 percent good-to-great, and the rest (64 percent) are passing the time or just plain toxic. I guess it really shouldn't come as a surprise . . . you could make an argument that those ratios probably hold true for nearly all workers.

If you have one of the good bosses, pinch yourself because you're one of the lucky ones. What does that mean for the other 64 percent of employees? It means you shouldn't pin all your hopes and dreams on someone who may be a nice-but-unenlightened boss to advance your career. Whatever your circumstances, you have to figure out a way to work through it. I think it is better to imagine you have an 87 percent chance of having a productive relationship with your boss—i.e., 36 percent <u>engaged</u> plus 51 percent <u>not engaged but not actively trying to sabotage your career either</u>. Let's assume the middle 51 percent are on the fence.

So what is an employee to do? My advice is to take control of your life. People at work don't love you like your family and best friends do. You can't rely on someone you barely know to care about you, your family, or your career. The stakes are too high. YOU need to be in charge of YOUR LIFE. Hoping and waiting for someone else to develop you, coach you, assign you the good projects, or promote you is not a good strategy. Think of your career as if you are playing the game of chess—your pieces are either attacking or being attacked—there is no middle ground. Do you want to take the initiative or be submissive?

FIND OUT WHAT IS IMPORTANT TO YOUR BOSS

It's important you are always aligned with your boss's expectations. Your goals and priorities should cascade from his goals and priorities. In this manner, your work activities will line up with what he wants you to be doing. Put yourself in your boss's shoes and try to understand what is important to him. (You can ask him directly, too.) Try to understand what his responsibilities and concerns are. If you do, you will be able to understand your boss and develop ways to distinguish yourself from others.

If you find yourself coming up with a great idea to improve productivity, work safer, or lower cost, approach your boss with your idea. Begin by talking about the problem or issue your co-workers are having and let your boss know you have some recommendations you would like to discuss in your next 1:1. When you communicate like this, you allow your boss adequate time to go through the short version of a Grief Cycle —i.e., shock, anger, depression, negotiation, and acceptance—which should increase the likelihood he will be receptive to your ideas by the time you meet.

BE PROACTIVE

If you have one of the good bosses (or even a *laissez-faire* one), I recommend you initiate the conversation about expectations. This is especially true when you first start a new position. It is always a good idea to ask your immediate supervisor what his expectations are, how he wants to be communicated with—i.e., in person, phone call, email, or text—and the frequency he wants to see status updates. His response may be to ask for a verbal update daily on the number of widgets you completed, or it could be a written weekly report. Regardless, I also recommend you schedule time to meet face to face regularly with your boss. As I have mentioned earlier, meeting 1:1 on a weekly or bi-weekly basis is best. If circumstances don't allow it—such as in cases where you work in different cities—at least try to schedule a formal phone call to speak with your boss at least once a month.

For those of you who work in the same building, you should use your 1:1 time as an opportunity to advance your ideas and to proactively let your boss know what you are doing. Walk him through the things you are doing, by priority, to make sure what you think is important aligns with what he thinks you should be doing.

Take the initiative to walk through your ideas about improving processes to lower cost, improve productivity, and grow sales. If you have a one-page template filled out for your 1:1 meeting, he will notice you are prepared, organized, and have your act together. Make two copies—one for you and one for him. I provided a sample 1:1 meeting template below that I've used for years. Feel free to rename or revise the template to match your needs. Add, modify, or delete sections weekly as necessary . . . and rename it to whatever works for you or fits your organization.

< Company Logo >	1:1 Weekly Planner		Date: 2/27/2019

GENERAL INFORMATION

PARTICIPANTS	ANNUAL REVIEW	CAREER DEVELOPMENT	DAY OFF / VAC
Employee:	Last:	Last:	Last:
Supervisor:	Next:	Next:	Next:

TRAVEL / CONFERENCES

PLANNED		DATE	COMMENTS	COST
1.				
2.				
3.				

OPERATIONAL PRIORITIES

INITIATIVE	NOTES

DISCUSSION ITEMS

1. Good news
2. Idea
3. Project update
4. Follow up |
5. Operational issue
6.

PROJECTS

PROJECT NAME	PCTG COMPLETE	COMMENTS / STATUS

CAREER DEVELOPMENT

STOP	
START	
CONTINUE	

Figure 8: 1:1 Meeting Agenda Template

Understanding Performance Reviews

Once you understand what your boss needs to accomplish to be successful, align your goals with his. Some organizations use a top-down approach to create and track performance goals. How performance reviews are administered differs from organization to organization. Oftentimes, larger companies establish quarterly (or annual) goals to measure your performance, which they use as criteria to evaluate your performance during annual reviews.

You should always have a running list of things you want to accomplish at work. I advise using quarterly goals, like the SMART goals described in Chapter 8. Constantly monitor your goals to make sure you are on track. If you must modify them, keep your boss informed as to why—and make sure you can defend your changes.

A word of caution. It is always prudent to set goals that are achievable but still allow you a little wiggle room. For example, if it's the beginning of the year and you've been assigned to a project your boss thinks should take six months to deliver, instead of stating, "I will complete Project Alpha by July 1," consider a Q1 goal of, "I will prepare the business case for Project Alpha by February 1 and, if approved by steering committee, kickoff the project by March 15." Believe me, in older/larger organizations, Murphy's Law prevails. Writing goals in this fashion affords you some leeway in case all new projects are put on a temporary hold, your business case presentation is rescheduled, or Murphy finds another way to ruin your plans.

If your performance review is due on your date of hire anniversary, start preparing for it about a month or two in advance. If you planned well, you should be able to cross out your list of "Goals" and write in the word "Accomplishments." Be prepared to elaborate on why you selected these goals. If you've already aligned with your boss, this should not be an issue. Quantify the benefit to the company wherever possible. For example, if you found a way to save storage costs by having the vendor ship equipment "just-in-time," then you should be able to calculate the savings. If you are in sales, you are a profit center. Don't be shy about explaining how you achieved 152 percent of your sales quota and added five new customers to long-term subscriptions.

To be realistic, most companies budget about a 3 percent merit pool every year. It's a zero-sum game too. In order to give one rising star a 5 percent raise, your boss will have to offset the larger raise by giving low performers a 1 or 2 percent raise. Everybody else pretty much gets 3 percent.

If you want a bigger raise, you must outperform your peers and be able to prove it. If you are a high performer and have been networking with peers in your industry (as you should be), you may occasionally get job offers to move to another company—maybe even a competitor. If you tell your boss about an offer in order to force their hand about giving you a raise or promotion, he can either present a counter offer if he wants you to stay . . . or not. Some bosses don't like to have a gun put to their head (figuratively speaking).

If your current employer can't or won't match your offer, you should be prepared for that. I don't recommend pulling the *offer* card unless you are prepared to leave the company. Without that kind of leverage, it's harder to convince your boss why you are an important contributor and should be paid more. By the way, this happened to me early in my career. In my situation, I got the raise. When I respectfully asked the president of the company, "If I was so valuable to the company, why didn't you pay me more before?" He told me, "If I don't *have to* pay more, why should I?" Businesses are in business to make money, not give it away.

There are no guarantees when it comes to getting raises. The best way to position yourself to make more money is to <u>be worth more</u> on the open job market (or have "leverage"). It is not unusual for IT and sales professionals to change companies several times throughout their careers. Each time they make a move, they get a promotion, a raise, or both. That may happen to you too, but only if you are a rainmaker and have a good reputation within your industry. By the way, the longer you are in a single industry, the more the world will shrink, the more everybody knows everybody . . . so nurture your reputation with care.

Staying
Successful

11 – PAY YOURSELF FIRST

"Someone's sitting in the shade today because
someone planted a tree a long time ago."
– Warren Buffet

This section is designed to help once you have landed a job and your career has begun. Now that you've become a profit center, we'll cover some basics like what to expect when it comes to your paycheck, how to create a budget so you don't spend more than you make, and how to save for your future.

Let's talk about take-home pay first. If you are a white-collar, salaried worker paid a rate of $800 per week and work forty hours for that pay period, then your paycheck will gross $800. If you work fifty hours one week—as a salaried worker—you will still only get paid $800. This is how office workers are usually paid. Therefore, *salaried* (or *exempt*) employees will receive a regular, fixed amount of pay regardless of the hours you put in.

Hourly (or *non-exempt*) workers, on the other hand, get paid by the hour. If you are making the same base rate—i.e., $20 per hour—and work forty hours, your gross pay will also be $800 per week. The difference is if you put in fifty hours one week, your paycheck will be $1,100 because non-exempt, hourly employees are eligible to receive overtime pay. Overtime (or OT) is calculated at 1.5 times your base rate for every hour you work that exceeds forty hours. Actually, how overtime is paid depends on the state and/or company you work for. Some companies pay OT for every hour over 8 hours per day while other companies won't pay overtime until you've accumulated at least forty hours in the work week.

Of the $800 gross pay you earned, Uncle Sam will withhold a percentage for federal taxes—the percentage depends on your tax bracket—and 7.65 percent for Social Security, which is also referred to as FICA (Federal Insurance Contributions Act). Depending on which state you live in, you may also have state income tax withheld. If your employer provides fringe benefits, you will have additional deductions for health insurance, dental insurance, vision insurance, and short-term and/or long-term disability insurance. How much those deductions are depends on the company you work for and how much they contribute to the cost. After all that, you might take home 65-70 percent of your gross earnings. Welcome to the world of being a W-2 employee. And we haven't even discussed whether your employer has a 401k plan or similar retirement savings program. In that case, you could have even more taken out of your check.

Now that you are a money-making machine, you need to make sure your income exceeds your expenses. Otherwise, you'll be broke before you know it! Let's assume you are leasing an apartment, so you'll have to pay rent. You'll definitely want to eat and have snacks handy. Ordering out for pizza once in a while is a given. Your closet is probably mostly empty, so you'll need to budget for some new clothes now and again. And you'll need to take care of yourself, so some of your newfound riches will be spent on soap, shampoo, toothpaste, and such.

All work and no play is a boring concept, right? If you want to go on a fun vacation, you'll need to start saving up for it now. If your research tells you the vacation will cost you $1,000, you need to figure out how much you can save per month until you have enough to go. Don't forget you may want to have some spending money and emergency cash for a rainy day.

Once you are living on your own—even if you have a roommate—you will have to provide for all your personal needs. Nobody else is going to do it, so you will have to learn to depend on yourself. If you want to go buy a pair of shoes, a business suit, or a dress, you will have to save up for it. The sooner you become responsible for yourself the better.

If you start out making $40k and save 10 percent of your take-home pay every week, by the end of one year, you could have saved about $3k. Don't touch it. That's your life savings. In fact, I recommend you put it in a different bank or credit union account than your regular checking account or whatever you use to pay your bills. Over time, you will be pleasantly surprised at how your money will grow.

Remember, you will pay for unexpected expenses in your lifetime. There will always be something like car troubles or your laptop will die or you'll have to buy a gift for your best friend's wedding. Worse yet, you or a loved one could get sick, so it would be wise to have some cash in a savings account for emergencies. Be smart and set aside some of your take-home pay from the very beginning so you learn how to live within your means.

By the way, I am <u>not</u> a financial advisor. The advice I offer here is very basic and only intended to help you save money and not get into debt over your head. In addition to your family and friends, which should be your first option, there are plenty of resources available so you can learn how to manage your money. In my humble opinion, I believe the books below should be recommended reading for those of you who are just starting out:

1.   *Complete Guide to Money,* by Dave Ramsey
2.   *Love Your Life Not Theirs: 7 Money Habits for Living the Life You Want,* by Rachel Cruze
3.   *Rich Dad, Poor Dad,* by Robert T. Kiyosaki

CREDIT CARDS

At some point, you will end up applying for a charge card or credit card. Having a credit card helps you establish and maintain a credit rating, and they are handy if you're ever in an emergency situation. Also, if you travel for work, you may need to have a credit card to charge business expenses with until you are reimbursed by your employer (if the company doesn't pay for all this for you in advance).

Personally, I prefer charge cards to credit cards because they force you to pay off the balance every month. If you can't afford it, then get a credit card . . . but don't go bonkers with it! Putting everything on credit with the intention of paying it off someday is foolish. Plain and simple, accumulating credit card debt is a bad idea. If you do have a charge card, maintain the discipline to pay off the balance every month or within a short period.

Don't accumulate debt. I have seen people charge everything on credit cards and then one day finding themselves unable to make the payments. Then they have to file for bankruptcy or work to pay interest expenses for years before they can dig themselves out of debt. If you get into trouble with credit cards, check out Dave Ramsey's snowball method for paying off debt.

BUDGETING

If you are living on your own, you need to put together a budget. Don't worry. Anybody who can add and subtract can create a budget. The budget itself isn't too hard. Having the discipline to adhere to it is the tough part. However, if you don't manage a budget, you won't have an organized way to ensure you spend less than you make. The most important thing to remember is to pay your bills on time, every time. Rent or mortgage is the most important; otherwise, you won't have a roof over your head. After food and toiletries, make sure you pay your car payment too. Missing rent or car payments will hurt your credit rating.

A good rule to live by is to pay your bills before you spend any money on discretionary spending like clothes, eating out, concerts, movies, or other optional spending (i.e., partying). The table below is a simple worksheet designed to help you understand what the elements of a basic budget looks like. Look through the line items to check how closely it matches your situation. Feel free to add or modify line items to fit your needs.

SAMPLE BUDGET

Based on a $40k salary

Category	Description	Amount
Income	Take-home pay	$ 2,233
Housing	Rent (apartment)	500
	Cable TV	40
	Internet	50
	Electricity	50
	Water	n/a
	Gas	n/a
	Cell phone	40
Food	Groceries, etc.	400
	Lunch money	150
Transportation	Car payment	200
	Car insurance	140
	Gasoline	90
Entertainment	Fun	200
Debt	Student loan	150
Savings	Pay yourself!	223
Total		$ 2,233
Balance		$ 0.00

Figure 9: Sample Budget

In this budget example, it assumes you are making an annual salary of $40,000. The Income line item is: $40k ÷ 12 months x 67 percent = $2,233 monthly take-home pay. In short, for this model, you'll take home 67 percent of your gross monthly pay.

I assume you are leasing an entry-level compact car and have to pay off student loans. In order to live in a nice, safe area, you have a roommate and are splitting the rent for an apartment. Over and above rent, I assume you will pay extra for utilities, internet access, and TV. (Make sure you ask about utility expenses before you sign a lease.) Speaking of leases, if you think you might get transferred for work or are in the military, make sure your apartment lease has a relocation clause so you can get out of your lease. If your lease has this clause, as long as you give a thirty-day notice and your relocation is greater than fifty miles away, you should be fine.

Even though the budget balance on the bottom line is $0.00, you are okay because you are still SAVING—because you are PAYING YOURSELF FIRST. If you get a raise, keep saving 10 percent of your take-home pay (or more if you can swing it) and try to live within your means. The more modestly you live when you're first starting out, the more money you will have for things that last like a home, weddings, or investments. If you blow too much money partying with your friends, you will always be broke. That said, there will always be a special occasion where you have to buy a new dress or rent a tuxedo. Just be smart about it.

VACATION ESCAPE CLAUSE

Time and money spent on vacations create lifelong memories. Conversely, money spent on foolishness is wasted forever, and if you make this a (bad) habit, you will be penniless. Having no money gets old fast. So make it worth your while. Plan for and save some money so you can travel to the places you've dreamed about.

Note: When you are saving for your vacation, that money shouldn't come out of your savings. Open another bank account and stash your vacation fund there. Fund it from the little sacrifices you make by saving money from another budget bucket, such as eating out, cutting back on clothing expenses, or finding ways to save on groceries. If you get an annual incentive check or holiday bonus, you can factor that into your vacation savings plan.

Touching your life savings for anything but a real emergency is verboten.

12 – CONTINUAL SELF-IMPROVEMENT

*"Make the most of yourself . . .
for that is all there is of you."*
– Ralph Waldo Emerson

When I was going through Infantry Basic Training in the US Army, I thought I would be learning all I needed to know to be a good soldier in the thirteen weeks I spent at Ft. Benning. In the beginning, the drill sergeants focused on general physical fitness—lots of running and calisthenics—then we learned the basics of marching and drills. Later, we learned how to shoot an M16 rifle, M40 recoilless rifle, LAW (Light Anti-Armor Weapon), and M203 grenade launcher. We also trained a little in hand-to-hand combat, studied land navigation, and practiced Nuclear- Biological-Chemical (NBC) attack readiness. However, it was not until I got to my first unit that I realized how much I still had to learn. It was during those first few months I learned to appreciate the older, more experienced veterans. It was humbling to realize they had forgotten more than I had ever learned.

After my enlistment in the Army ended, I enrolled at a local community college and soon discovered the same axioms applied to education. Taking a Finance 101 college course only teaches the fundamentals of finance. What I learned in class was all academic until I got the chance to apply what I learned. As an older student, this turned out to be an advantage for me. One evening I would learn how to calculate Return on Investment (ROI), and the next day, I would go to work and write up the business case for a new project.

Then one day at work, I was asked to be the lead on a proposal my company was making to do the design, engineering, and build for a next-generation Corvette prototype. I was pretty excited but knew it was going to be a lot of work. With the help of our executive team, I wrote marketing copy outlining our engineering services and capabilities then had to respond to a litany of questions in the Request For Proposal (RFP). To develop our pricing structure, I had to calculate all our anticipated costs, mark-up, and our payback period or NPV (Net Present Value) and include this cost justification in the proposal.

The cool part is we won the bid! It was a $25 million program and that put a nice, fluffy feather in my cap for having played a big part. The moral of the story is, especially for those who are changing careers or going back to school, there is an upside to it. You may get the chance to gain practical experience at work to apply what you learn in school at night!

My point in telling you this is attending trade school or university only provides you with some fundamental concepts in your chosen occupation. Earning a bachelor's degree is the equivalent of graduating military *basic training*. Becoming an EXPERT is something you need to work on continuously to distinguish yourself from the rest.

> *"Formal education will make you a living;*
> *self-education will make you a fortune."*
> *– Jim Rohn*

Continuing to invest in yourself is the most important thing you can do. Constantly learning and growing gives you the best chance to sustain a positive career trajectory. There is only one you, so make the most of what skills and motivation you already have by staying the course. Become an avid reader and master your profession to the extent you can confidently say to yourself you know your trade inside and out.

Find out who is the best at your profession—i.e., the "experts"—and try to network with them. Most people are happy to share their story about how they got where they are. Do this and take all the additional training you can. Earn professional certifications, join local organizations, and never stop learning. If you do these things, you are giving yourself the best chance to become one of the experts yourself.

Learning is a lifelong thing. After you graduate with a trade cert or college degree, you are not done. Thinking like that can lead you to end up with a career stuck in neutral. Somebody, somewhere— i.e., your competition—will outwork you, and if they are reading trade journals, attending conferences, and networking . . . they are going to pass you by.

Talk with the most successful people in your field, and you'll find they constantly learn. Almost every career field has a professional organization. If your organization has a local chapter, get involved in it and become a contributor—or even a chapter officer. Commit to continuously learn—by reading, listening to audiobooks on your drive to and from work, or taking online courses. Earn relevant certifications to augment your credentials where possible.

If you are part of a large organization and are competing for a promotion with a few others, ask yourself how you are perceived among your peers and with your leadership. How do you look on paper? Does your resume, credentials, experience, and education stack up?

If you have similar experience and education with a rival, having professional certifications or being involved in a local trade organization may tip the odds in your favor. As a former recruiter and executive who evaluated talent, I recommend you give yourself every advantage possible.

PEOPLE SKILLS

If you don't master the art of building relationships with co-workers and colleagues, you will severely handicap your potential for success. Think of it as developing a network of friends who have a common interest, you. If you help them be successful and achieve their goals, then chances are they will help you when you need them. The more you give, the more you gain.

For those of you who may be on a bit of the shy side, you may find it a little difficult to reach out to others for help. Needing help isn't a sign of weakness. Rather, it is a sign of strength. Besides, most people like to help others, and if you don't ask, you'll be depriving someone who'd love an opportunity to serve.

Building a strong network of like-minded people affords everyone a sounding board to bounce ideas off of each other. This can help you all—both professionally and personally. Look at the most successful people out there. Did they do everything by themselves? No, of course not.

We can't achieve greatness alone. Build your alliances, and you will discover how much more is possible. Just keep pushing on . . . It's your edge.

Nothing in the world can take the place of perseverance.
Talent will not;
Nothing is more common than unsuccessful people with talent.
Genius will not;
Unrewarded genius is almost legendary;
Education will not;
The world is full of educated derelicts.
Perseverance and Determination alone are omnipotent."
– Calvin Coolidge

CHANGING CAREERS

If you think your time has passed or it is too late for you to make a change, you are wrong. If you are still breathing, you have the POWER to change your life. You are not defeated. People over forty and fifty years old have re-invented themselves and found success and happiness. Just think how much smarter you are now than when you were younger. All the missteps of the past are ones you will not repeat, so in actuality, your path should be shorter. The older you get, you will find it isn't the failures you regret most . . . it will be the things you didn't at least try.

Life is precious. You need to decide what you want to do with your life and go for it. Think of the proudest moments in your life. Was it when you had to work your butt off to achieve a goal and achieved it? Or when you won $100 in a scratch-off lottery ticket?

I get a little sad when I think of the people I have known in my life who I believe could have been great but never tried. Do you know anyone who talked about their dream but never got off the couch to chase it?

Colonel Harland David Sanders took a chance at sixty-five years old. He traveled across the country trying to sell franchise rights to restaurant owners for his chicken recipe. Legend says he was rejected 1,009 times before he got his first *yes* that paid him a nickel for every piece of chicken the restaurant sold. Eventually, *Kentucky Fried Chicken* (a.k.a. KFC) was born, and Colonel Sanders became world famous.

J.K. Rowling lost her mother to multiple sclerosis. Later in life, she got married, suffered a miscarriage, got divorced, and was a single mother. Jobless, penniless, and diagnosed with depression, she considered suicide. Rowling's manuscript was rejected by a dozen publishers. After a year of trying, Bloombury finally published her first book, *Harry Potter and the Philosopher's Stone*. Within five years, she went from an impoverished single mother on welfare to become one of the richest women in the world!

Every day you make choices. Your path in life is determined by the decisions you make every day. One day, your choice could be as simple as whether or not to say hello to a stranger in the park. What if you struck up a conversation? What if you later developed a friendship . . . and that friendship eventually led you to become partners in a business venture that made you both very wealthy. Not a bad choice that day, eh? On the other hand, what if you had avoided him and just walked by without saying anything that day?

Don't be afraid to act. People who are self-made and have found success had the intestinal fortitude to go after their dreams. They did not give up despite all of the challenges life threw at them. Every day and everyone who crosses your path represents an opportunity. Will you smile and say hello?

What you decide to do with this gift called life is up to you.

READING LIST

Reading expands your mind and triggers thoughts that can change your life. For what it's worth, I have provided a list of books that have made an impact on me and influenced how I approach my career planning and management. There are many more books out there that can inspire you. I urge you to broaden your mind by taking in new information. Continuously grow throughout your life. I hope you enjoy these books as much as I have.

1. *The Power of Ambition: Unleashing the Conquering Drive Within You!* by Jim Rohn
2. *The Richest Man in Babylon* by George S. Clason & Grover Gardner
3. *How to Win Friends and Influence People* by Dale Carnegie
4. *The 7 Habits of Highly Effective People* by Stephen Covey
5. *Think and Grow Rich* by Napoleon Hill
6. *Winning Every Day: The Game Plan for Success* by Lou Holtz
7. *The Definitive Book of Body Language* by Allan & Barbara Pease
8. *Getting More: How to Negotiate to Achieve Your Goals in the Real World* by Stuart Diamond
9. *Customers for Life* by Carl Sewell
10. *The Speed of Trust* by Stephen Covey
11. *The Storyteller's Secret: From TED Speakers to Business Legends, Why Some Ideas Catch On and Others Don't* by Carmine Gallo
12. *Everyone Communicates—Few Connect* by John C. Maxwell
13. *Who Moved My Cheese* by Spencer Johnson, M.D.
14. *How the World Sees You* by Sally Hogshead
15. *StrengthsFinder 2.0* by Tom Rath
16. *StandOut 2.0* by Marcus Buckingham
17. *Siddhartha,* by Hermann Hesse

WORKS CITED

Evans, Will. You have 6 seconds to make an impression: How recruiters see your resume. March 12, 2012, <https://www.theladders.com/career-advice/you-only-get-6-seconds-of-fame-make-it-count>

Doyle, Allisonn. Top 10 Job Interview Questions and Best Answers. February 3, 2019, <https://www.thebalancecareers.com/top-interview-questions-and-best-answers-2061225>

How to Answer the 31 Most Common Interview Questions. https://www.themuse.com/advice/how-to-answer-the-31-most-common-interview-questions

Covey, Steven. 7 Habits of Highly Successful People. New York: Free Press, 2004. Print.

Diamond, Stuart. Getting More: How to Negotiate to Achieve Your Goals in the Real World. New York: Crown Publishing Group, 2010. Print.

Carnegie, Dale, 1888-1955. How To Win Friends and Influence People. New York: Simon & Schuster, 2009. Print.

Belludi, Nagesh. Albert Mehrabian's 7-38-55 Rule of Personal Communication. October 4, 2008, <http://www.rightattitudes.com/2008/10/04/7-38-55-rule-personal-communication/>

Schawbel, Dan. 14 Things Every Successful Person Has in Common, Forbes, <https://www.forbes.com/sites/danschawbel/2013/12/17/14-things-every-successful-person-has-in-common/#449612133c74>

Mulder, Patty. SMART Goals. ToolsHero, <https://www.toolshero.com/time-management/smart-goals/>

Patel, Sujan. 10 Behaviors of Unsuccessful People, Inc., July 19, 2016, <https://www.inc.com/sujan-patel/10-behaviors-of-unsuccessful-people.html>

Sewell, Carl. Customers for Life: How to Turn That One-Time Buyer into a Lifetime Customer. New York: Doubleday, 1998. Print.

Harter, Jim and Rigoni, Brandon. The State of the American Manager. Gallup, Inc., <https://integraladvisors.com/wp-content/uploads/2013/02/State-Of-the-American-Manager.pdf>

McLeod, Lea. 10 Ways to Get Your Boss to Trust You Completely. The Muse, <https://www.themuse.com/advice/10-ways-to-get-your-boss-to-trust-you-completely>